Paragraphs
for
Middle School

A Sentence-Composing Approach

A Student Worktext

Don and Jenny Killgallon

HEINEMANN
Portsmouth, NH

Heinemann
361 Hanover Street
Portsmouth, NH 03801–3912
www.heinemann.com

Offices and agents throughout the world

Library of Congress Cataloging-in-Publication Data
Killgallon, Don.
    Paragraphs for middle school : a sentence-composing approach : a student worktext / Don and Jenny Killgallon.
       p. cm.
    Includes bibliographical references.
    ISBN-13: 978-0-325-04268-8
    ISBN-10: 0-325-04268-3
    1. English language—Sentences.   2. English language—Composition and exercises.   3. English language—Rhetoric.   I. Killgallon, Jenny.   II. Title.
PE1441.K46 2013
372.62'3044—dc23   2012040350

Editor: Tobey Antao
Production: Victoria Merecki
Interior and cover designs: Monica Ann Crigler
Typesetter: Cape Cod Compositors, Inc.
Manufacturing: Steve Bernier

Printed in the United States of America on acid-free paper
22   21   20   19   18   PPC   4   5   6   7   8

Deep and wide thanks to my brother Joe, my mentor in so many ways, for opening the door to my profession: teaching English. Without him, this book—and all the others—wouldn't exist.

—Don

CONTENTS

THE SENTENCE-COMPOSING APPROACH

The more the writer knows about his or her tools and the more practice in using them, the more expert the student writer becomes at using those tools in crafting words, phrases, sentences, paragraphs.

—Constance Weaver, *Grammar to Enrich & Enhance Writing*

THE SENTENCE–PARAGRAPH LINK   1

Sentences unfold one part at a time. Paragraphs unfold one sentence at a time. In this section, authors become your invisible teachers in an apprenticeship in the sentence-composing approach to building better sentences for better paragraphs.

BUILDING BETTER SENTENCES

BEST SENTENCES   3

A sentence must have a subject (topic) and a predicate (comment about the topic). Best sentences always have something even more important: sentence parts that are tools to build better sentences like those written by authors.

IMITATING SENTENCES   14

Imitating how authors build their sentences focuses on how they write and helps you write in similar ways. It is like filling in pictures in a coloring book. When you color a picture, you're given the shape for the picture, and you add your own colors. When you imitate a sentence, you're given the shape for the sentence, and you add your own words.

SENTENCE-COMPOSING TOOLS

Writing is carpentry with sentences and paragraphs. Like any craft, it is only as good as the plans, materials, and tools you use. Here you will learn, practice, and use tools that foster elaboration in paragraphs. All of them are used frequently by your mentor-authors, who will guide you in learning how to use them in your own writing.

TOOL PLACES

Putting things in the right places requires skill, whether in your room, your locker, or your sentences. When you learn where authors place their sentence-composing tools, in your sentences you'll skillfully put things in the right places.

THE OPENER

This place is up front, in the beginning of a sentence.

THE S-V SPLIT

This place is between the subject and its verb.

THE CLOSER

This place is way back, at the end of a sentence.

THE MIX

This place is several different places in the same sentence.

REVIEW OF TOOLS

They're all here: openers, S-V splits, closers, and mixes.

OUT OF BOUNDS   122

Sentences need clear boundaries to tell your readers where one sentence ends and the next sentence begins. In this section, you'll study how careless writers sometimes go "out of bounds" by writing too much sentence, or too little. You'll learn to detect, eliminate, and avoid three sentence boundary problems: the fragment, the comma splice, and the run-on.

BUILDING BETTER PARAGRAPHS

BEST PARAGRAPHS   139

A paragraph contains two or more sentences linked because they are about the same topic. Best paragraphs always have something else: sentence-composing tools like the ones used by authors.

EXPANDING PARAGRAPHS   144

Learning how authors add details and imitating what they do will strengthen your writing. Here, you'll partner with authors to create well-built paragraphs by using the sentence-composing tools you learned earlier and achieve one of the most important qualities of good writing: elaboration.

IMITATING PARAGRAPHS   161

Activities here help you learn how to compose better paragraphs by imitating the experts. Model paragraphs by authors give you a blueprint for composing your own well-built paragraphs.

UNSCRAMBLING PARAGRAPHS   181

Good paragraphs arrange content in ways that make sense to your readers. Unscrambling paragraphs to produce a meaningful arrangement is good practice for composing coherent paragraphs.

BUILDING PARAGRAPHS   192

In these activities, you'll practice creating and placing additions effectively within paragraphs to make them stronger.

YOUR INVISIBLE TEACHERS   206

Over four hundred sources are the basis for the activities in *Paragraphs for Middle School: A Sentence-Composing Approach*. Included are model sentences and paragraphs from hundreds of authors—your silent mentors, your invisible teachers.

WITH GRATITUDE

Thanks to the hundreds of authors within—your mentors in this apprenticeship in sentence composing for better paragraphs—for modeling good writing and showing you the way to better writing through imitation to creation.

To help you achieve mastery as a writer, you'll find lots of activities within these pages for practicing how good writers build strong sentences and paragraphs. You'll imitate how they do it, and eventually—as a result of practicing what they do—build strong sentences and paragraphs on your own.

PRACTICING: To achieve mastery the student must read widely and deeply and must write not just carefully but continually, thoughtfully assessing and reassessing what he or she writes, because practice, for the writer as for the concert pianist, is the heart of the matter.

—John Gardner, *The Art of Fiction: Notes on Craft for Young Writers*

THE SENTENCE–PARAGRAPH LINK

Much of good writing is a process of addition. Good writers say more. Often, students don't write better because they don't have the tools for elaboration.

A major goal of *Paragraphs for Middle School: A Sentence-Composing Approach* is to provide tools for elaboration within sentences and paragraphs.

Contrast these two paragraphs to see the dramatic difference in elaboration the underlined tools make:

BASIC PARAGRAPH

A twelve-year-old boy sat up in bed. There was a sound coming from outside. It was a huge, heavy rush. It was coming from directly above the house. The boy swung his legs off the bed. The yard was otherworldly. The boy stood on the lawn.

ELABORATE PARAGRAPH

In the predawn darkness, in the back bedroom of a small house in Torrance, California, a twelve-year-old boy sat up in bed, listening. There was a sound coming from outside, growing ever louder. It was a huge, heavy rush, suggesting immensity, a great parting of air. It was coming from directly above the house. The boy swung his legs off the bed, raced down the stairs, slapped open the back door, and loped onto the grass. The yard was otherworldly, smothered in unnatural darkness, shivering with sound. The boy stood on the lawn, head thrown back, spellbound.

Laura Hillenbrand, *Unbroken*

The underlined parts are the result of the author's use of sentence-composing tools that create additions for elaboration. Here's good news:

You can own the same tools authors use to build sentences to add elaboration for their paragraphs.

Paragraphs for Middle School: A Sentence-Composing Approach teaches imitation of real sentences and paragraphs, worthy models by hundreds of authors. With this approach, with only a single sentence or paragraph as a manageable model, and with frequent imitation through varied activities, you can succeed, often astonishingly, in writing sentences and paragraphs like those of authors.

Words are the raw materials of writing. All sentences are made up of words. All paragraphs are made up of sentences. What makes the writing of effective writers different from the writing of ineffective writers? The answer is how those words, sentences, and paragraphs are shaped and styled.

In this worktext, *Paragraphs for Middle School: A Sentence-Composing Approach*, you'll see how over four hundred authors shaped and styled their sentences and paragraphs, and, through the many activities using those sentences and paragraphs, how you can similarly shape and style your own sentences and paragraphs. Those authors are your invisible teachers.

Through their sentences and their paragraphs, those hundreds of authors are ready to teach you the essential link between good sentences and good paragraphs.

I threw words all over the place
and none of them landed right.

—Pat Conroy, *My Reading Life*

Learn everything you can from your teachers, visible and invisible, as they go about the important work of teaching you how to build better sentences and paragraphs. If you do, your words will land right.

BEST SENTENCES

Lists of "bests" recommend what to buy, see, read, view, hear, wear, visit, and so forth. What about writing? A helpful way to improve your writing is to study the best practices of good writers, namely, authors whose writing is widely read and appreciated.

This book focuses on those best practices, zooming in on the basic component of writing: the sentence. Learning how authors write "best sentences" for paragraphs is the purpose of this book, with activities and assignments to help you build better sentences, and, through those sentences, better paragraphs, and, through those paragraphs, better stories, essays, and reports.

What are "best sentences"? This section answers that question by demonstrating that they are sentences made up of three parts: subjects, predicates, and—the most important—tools.

THE MUST-HAVES: A SUBJECT AND A PREDICATE

Two sentence parts are absolutely necessary for a complete sentence: a subject and a predicate.

A sentence tells people something about a topic. The topic is called the subject of the sentence. The comment about the topic is called the predicate.

These are just topics, not part of a sentence yet.

1. The clumsy kid

2. A desktop full of computer stuff

3. Big Al with his quarterback shoulders

4. Surfing the Internet

5. Typing slowly to make fewer mistakes

6. To earn money to buy something he wanted

7. What Geraldo enjoyed after school

8. Tisha's interview of the principal

9. Janine's new hairstyle

10. The last round of the spelling bee

These are just comments, not part of a sentence yet.

1. tripped over his shoelace

2. cluttered Troy's room

3. was featured in the sports section of the newspaper

4. got out of hand and took up too much time

5. turned out to be a good idea

6. was why Alfredo looked for a job

7. was a session with friends

8. was in the school newspaper

9. suited her new clothes

10. resulted in a win for our team

How do you write a complete sentence? Put the ten topics and ten comments about those topics together to make ten complete sentences. Now each sentence has the two sentence parts every sentence needs: a subject and a predicate.

SUBJECT (topic)	PREDICATE (comment about the topic)
The clumsy kid	tripped over his shoelace.
A desktop full of computer stuff	cluttered Troy's room.
Big Al with his quarterback shoulders	was featured in the sports section of the newspaper.
Surfing the Internet	got out of hand and took up too much time.
Typing slowly to make fewer mistakes	turned out to be a good idea.
To earn money to buy something he wanted	was why Alfredo looked for a job.
What Geraldo enjoyed after school	was a session with friends.
Tisha's interview of the principal	was in the school newspaper.
Janine's new hairstyle	suited her new clothes.
The last round of the spelling bee	resulted in a win for our school.

ACTIVITY 1: CREATING SUBJECTS

Some sentences have the same subject but different predicates. Make up your own subject and use it in five sentences with different predicates.

EXAMPLES

1. The cat in the tree leaped from the branch.
2. The cat in the tree meowed.
3. The cat in the tree looked frightened.
4. The cat in the tree clung to the limb.
5. The cat in the tree swallowed a bird.

ACTIVITY 2: CREATING PREDICATES

Some sentences have the same predicate but different subjects. Make up your own predicate and use it in five sentences with different subjects.

EXAMPLES

1. The kids who ate the worms <u>burst out laughing</u>.

2. Frank, Bobo, and Maura <u>burst out laughing</u>.

3. After the joke, Kander <u>burst out laughing</u>.

4. During the speech in front of the room, Blair <u>burst out laughing</u>.

5. Looking at the purple pizza, the customer <u>burst out laughing</u>.

ACTIVITY 3: MATCHING

Match the subject with its predicate to make a sentence. Write out each sentence, underlining the subject once, and the predicate twice.

Subjects	Predicates
1. The wounded from this morning's bombing ^ . Suzanne Collins, *Mockingjay*	a. hung in the smoke-house
2. The meat, dry-cured for the feeding of the dogs, ^ . Marjorie Kinnan Rawlings, *The Yearling*	b. meant trouble and danger
3. Spraying bright colors, dancing, and singing, ^ . Charles R. Joy, "Hindu Girl of Surinam"	c. were being brought in, on homemade stretchers, in wheelbarrows, on carts
4. Whoever had worn those sneakers ^ . Louis Sachar, *Holes*	d. had a bad case of foot odor
5. To get his feet wet in such a freezing temperature ^ . Jack London, "To Build a Fire"	e. are all part of the excitement

Sometimes sentences have more than one subject. Those sentences say something about more than one topic.

EXAMPLES

1. <u>The fierce black eyes of the man</u> and <u>the laughing blue eyes of the goose girl</u> met across the strip of swamp. (*two subjects with same predicate*)

    Elinor Mordaunt, "The Prince and the Goose Girl"

2. <u>Driving snow</u>, <u>a wind that cut like a hot knife</u>, and <u>darkness</u> forced them to look for a camping place. (*three subjects with same predicate*)

    Jack London, *The Call of the Wild*

3. <u>The wicked eyes</u>, <u>the ancient face</u>, <u>the fierce look</u>, <u>the enormous size of the two-and-a-half-ton hippo</u> required very rapid action. (*four subjects with same predicate*)

    Leon Hugo, "My Father and the Hippopotamus"

Sometimes sentences have more than one predicate. Those sentences say more than one thing about the subject.

EXAMPLES

1. The tiny dragon <u>lost interest in Eragon</u> and <u>awkwardly explored the room</u>. (*two predicates with one subject*)

    Christopher Paolini, *Eragon*

2. He <u>felt something cold on his ankles</u> and <u>looked under the tablecloth</u> and <u>saw two more of the huge worms around his ankles</u>. (*three predicates with one subject*)

    Thomas Rockwell, *How to Eat Fried Worms*

3. One of the creatures high above the trees <u>raised its head to listen</u>, then <u>flew off</u>, <u>picked three flowers from a tree growing near the river</u>, and <u>brought them over to the children</u>. (*four predicates with one subject*)

    Madeleine L'Engle, *A Wrinkle in Time*

- -

Sometimes sentences have more than one subject and more than one predicate. Those sentences say more than one thing about more than one subject.

EXAMPLES

1. <u>She</u> and <u>her father</u> <u>unrolled the paper across the kitchen</u> and <u>knelt with a box of crayons between them</u>. (*two subjects and two predicates*)

    Beverly Cleary, *Ramona and Her Father*

2. <u>The tall skinny Bean</u> and <u>the dwarfish pot-bellied Bunce</u> <u>drove their machines like maniacs</u>, <u>raced the motors</u>, and <u>made the shovels dig at a terrific speed</u>. (*two subjects and three predicates*)

    Roald Dahl, *Fantastic Mr. Fox*

3. <u>The four children</u> and <u>the Dwarf</u> <u>went down to the water's edge</u>, <u>pushed off the boat with some difficulty</u>, and <u>scrambled aboard</u>. (*two subjects and three predicates*)

C. S. Lewis, The Chronicles of Narnia

ACTIVITY 4: EXPANDING

At the caret mark (^), expand the sentence. For sentences 1–5, add subjects, for 6–10, predicates, for 11–15, both subjects and predicates. Make up content that blends well in content and style with the rest of the author's sentence.

ADD SUBJECTS

1. ^ burst into tears, knowing that in the picture her eyes would look very puffy indeed.

Ann Brashares, Girls in Pants

2. ^ was bent outward at an awkward angle from the leg, his trousers flattened, soaked in blood.

Michael Crichton, Jurassic Park

3. ^ was standing there all red-faced, screaming and waving his arms around.

Kate DiCamillo, Because of Winn-Dixie

4. Smoothing out the yellowed newspaper for the thousandth time, ^ scanned the page, hoping to find some bit of news about my daddy.

Clare Vanderpool, Moon Over Manifest

5. For perhaps fifteen seconds, ^ and ^ examined each other, with the scrutiny of those who take chances with life and death.

F. R. Buckley, "Gold-Mounted Guns"

ADD PREDICATES

6. The huge head of the tyrannosaur ^ .

Michael Crichton, *Jurassic Park*

7. One of the rocks, black and sharp, like an ugly tooth, ^ .

Franklin W. Dixon, *The Hardy Boys: The House on the Cliff*

8. Walking back toward the patrol car, the policeman ^ and ^ .

Carl Hiaasen, *Hoot*

9. He remained on the floor and ^ and ^ .

Robert Cormier, *Take Me Where the Good Times Are*

10. The wizard folded up the letter with a sigh, ^ , ^ , and ^ .

J. K. Rowling, *Harry Potter and the Chamber of Secrets*

ADD SUBJECTS AND PREDICATES

11. ^ and I just ^ and fell upon the floor.

Mildred D. Taylor, *Roll of Thunder, Hear My Cry*

12. At the front door Mother and Father and ^ and ^ bowed and ^ .

Monica Sone, "The Japanese Touch"

13. Whenever the wind came through the sky, he and ^ would sit in the stone hut and ^ .

Ray Bradbury, *The Martian Chronicles*

14.   ^ , computer printouts, forbiddingly thick bound documents cover the mayor's desk, and ^ .

> Tracy Kidder, *Home Town*

15.   ^ grabbed ink bottles and sprayed the class with them, ^ , ^ , ^ , ^ , and ^ .

> J. K. Rowling, *Harry Potter and the Chamber of Secrets*

REVIEW

Every sentence must have at least one subject and at least one predicate.

SUBJECT FACTS	
1. Subjects can be at the very beginning of the sentence.	**The children** came charging back into their homeroom. Rosa Guy, *The Friends*
2. Subjects can be even at the end.	Swinging down the valley on long pointed wings was **a large bird**. Jean Craighead George, *My Side of the Mountain*
3. Subjects can be long.	**The huge eye on the right side of the monster's anguished head** glittered before me like a cauldron. Ray Bradbury, "The Fog Horn"
4. Subjects can be short.	**Flies** buzzed in through the door, landing on the open watermelons and the sweet corn. Robert Lipsyte, *The Contender*
5. Subjects can do just one thing.	**Malcolm** raced with his feet splashing in the mud. Michael Crichton, *Jurassic Park*

6. Subjects can do more than one thing.	**Malcolm** twisted the handle, kicked open the door, and ran. Michael Crichton, *Jurassic Park*
7. Sentences can have just one subject.	Nearby, **a white horse** cropped the grass. Lloyd Alexander, *The Book of Three*
8. Sentences can have more than one subject.	**The gloom, the chill, and the creeping mist in this strange and bewildering land** were almost too much. Alexander Key, *The Forgotten Door*
9. Sentences must have a subject—or they won't make sense! *Without a subject, we don't know who tackled Charles Wallace.*	**(no subject) ?** tackled Charles Wallace as though he were a football. Madeleine L'Engle, *A Wrinkle in Time*

PREDICATE FACTS

1. Predicates usually come after the subject.	His legs **looked like telephone poles**. Robert Lipsyte, *The Contender*
2. Predicates sometimes come before the subject.	**In front of one of the houses stood** a little boy with a ball Madeleine L'Engle, *A Wrinkle in Time*
3. Predicates can be short.	Overhead, the branches **rustled**. Lloyd Alexander, *The Book of Three*
4. Predicates can be long.	Nearby, on an orange crate, he **set out bottles of ketchup and Worcestershire sauce, jars of piccalilli and mustard, a box of crackers, salt and pepper shakers, a lemon, a slice of cheese, his mother's tin cinnamon-and-sugar shaker, a box of Kleenex, a jar of maraschino cherries, some horseradish, and a plastic honey bear**. Thomas Rockwell, *How to Eat Fried Worms*

5. Predicates can tell just one thing.

He **tugged at the locked door handle**.
Michael Crichton, *Jurassic Park*

6. Predicates can tell more than one thing.

He **raised one eyebrow, stared at me for five seconds, stomped to the recliner and sat down on the very edge with his back ramrod straight.**
Stephenie Meyer, *Breaking Dawn*

7. Sentences must have predicates—or they won't make sense!

Without a predicate, we don't know what the social studies teacher did.

(Here's the answer, a predicate: **growled at me to sit down in the auditorium.**)

My social studies teacher **?** **(no predicate)**
Laurie Halse Anderson, *Speak*

IMITATING SENTENCES

What are some things you learned to do by watching other people do them—like hammering a nail or threading a needle, making pancakes, buttoning your shirt or blouse, swinging a bat or tennis racket? How did you learn these and other things? You probably learned by watching people and then imitating what they did.

You can learn how to write sentences like ones by famous authors of stories by imitating authors who know—really, really know—how to build great sentences. They include authors like Suzanne Collins (*The Hunger Games*), Michael Crichton (*Jurassic Park*), C. S. Lewis (*The Chronicles of Narnia*), Sarah Dessen (*Dreamland*), Rick Riordan (*The Lightning Thief*), and J. K. Rowling (Harry Potter novels), plus many others whose sentences are in this worktext to teach you to build great sentences like theirs. Those authors are your invisible teachers.

Imitating sentences is like filling in a picture in a coloring book. When you color a picture, you're given the shape for the picture, and you add your own colors. When you imitate a sentence, you're given the shape for the sentence, and you add your own words. In the following practices, you'll learn how to imitate great sentences.

ACTIVITY 1: CHUNKING

People read and write sentences one sentence part at a time. Each sentence part is a "chunk" of meaning in the sentence. Read each pair of sentences a chunk (sentence part) at a time. Copy the sentence that makes sense because it is divided into meaningful chunks.

EXAMPLE

Sentences

a. At the entrance / to the Peace Park, / people filed through the memorial building / in silence.

b. At the /entrance to the Peace / Park, people filed through the memorial / building in silence.

Eleanor Coerr, Sadako and the Thousand Paper Cranes

CORRECT: **a**

- -

1a. Harold has been a / friend of / mine, one of the few in the / village my age.

1b. Harold has been / a friend of mine, / one of the few / in the village my age.

Carrie Ryan, The Forest of Hands and Teeth

2a. To my right is Gretchen, / who's got her chin jutting out / as if it would win the race / all by itself.

2b. To my right is Gretchen, who's / got her chin jutting out as / if it would win the race all / by itself.

Toni Cade Bambara, "Raymond's Run"

3a. At the window with / his crippled foot propped on / a pillow, Romey reported smoke coming from the / chimney of Kiser's / house.

3b. At the window / with his crippled foot / propped on a pillow, Romey reported smoke / coming from the chimney / of Kiser's house.

Bill and Vera Cleaver, Where the Lilies Bloom

4a. She moved with / lightning swiftness, striking out at / him with her open hand, making a / blow to his chest that would have / sent him down gasping if he'd / been a human being.

4b. She moved with lightning swiftness, / striking out at him / with her open hand, / making a blow to his chest / that would have sent him down gasping / if he'd been a human being.

Cassandra Clare, City of Bones

5a. After the tyrannosaur's head crashed / against the hood of the Land Cruiser / and shattered the windshield, Tim was knocked flat / on the seat, / blinking in the darkness, / his mouth warm with blood.

5b. After the tyrannosaur's / head crashed against the hood of the / Land Cruiser and shattered the windshield, Tim was / knocked flat on the seat, blinking in the / darkness, his / mouth warm with blood.

Michael Crichton, Jurassic Park

Do for HW

ACTIVITY 2: MATCHING IMITATIONS

Match the imitation sentence with its model sentence.

Model Sentences	Imitation Sentences
1. Harold has been a friend of mine, one of the few in the village my age. Carrie Ryan, *The Forest of Hands and Teeth*	**a.** In front of me is Nathan, who's got his arms flailing around as if he were a living windmill standing all alone.
2. To my right is Gretchen, who's got her chin jutting out as if it would win the race all by itself. Toni Cade Bambara, "Raymond's Run"	**b.** Reggie was always a favorite of hers, one of the relatives in her family her equal.
3. At the window with his crippled foot propped on a pillow, Romey reported smoke coming from the chimney of Kiser's house. Bill and Vera Cleaver, *Where the Lilies Bloom*	**c.** He leapt with astonishing lightness, moving away from his attacker with his nimble legs, escaping a punch to his stomach that would have taken him down struggling if he'd been a slower reactor.
4. She moved with lightning swiftness, striking out at him with her open hand, making a blow to his chest that would have sent him down gasping if he'd been a human being. Cassandra Clare, *City of Bones*	**d.** After the little kid walked around the edge of the double bed and saw the puppy, he was stopped cold in his tracks, staring at the dog, his eyes wide with delight.

5. After the tyrannosaur's head crashed against the hood of the Land Cruiser and shattered the windshield, Tim was knocked flat on the seat, blinking in the darkness, his mouth warm with blood. Michael Crichton, *Jurassic Park*	**e.** In the bleachers with his bandaged elbow secured in a sling, Liam cheered baskets scored by the home team of his high school.

ACTIVITY 3: UNSCRAMBLING IMITATIONS

Unscramble and write out the sentence parts to imitate the model sentence. Then write your own sentence imitation with sentence parts like the model. Write about something from your imagination or from a TV show, movie, story, or book.

EXAMPLE

Model Sentence: Sara watched him as he walked, a small figure for his ten years, wearing faded blue jeans and a striped knit shirt that was stretched out of shape.

Betsy Byars, *The Summer of the Swans*

Scrambled Sentence Parts

a. a graceful dancer in her teenage years

b. and matching pink leotard that was chosen for that dance

c. wearing hot pink tights

d. Tina admired the performer as she watched

Unscrambled Imitation: Tina admired the performer as she watched, a graceful dancer in her teenage years, wearing hot pink tights and matching pink leotard that was chosen for that dance.

Sample Student Imitation: The crowd applauded the champion as she performed, a skillful gymnast in the Olympics, demonstrating incredible vaulting and balance beam moves that were timed perfectly in sync.

- -

1. He carried the book with him in one hand, the pistol ready in his other.

Ray Bradbury, The Martian Chronicles

    1a. on a plate

    1b. the drink steady on her tray

    1c. Clarissa took the sandwich with her

2. Putting a hand to my forehead, I felt a welt and a crust of hardened blood.

Avi, Crispin: The Cross of Lead

    2a. and a hint of sweet molasses

    2b. Teagan smelled ginger

    2c. putting his nose to the cookie

3. The sun was just beginning to drive its first splinters of light through the pines, bouncing against tree trunks and earth.

William H. Armstrong, Sounder

    3a. passing through the rose garden and lavender

    3b. through the air

    3c. to waft its alluring scents of freshness

    3d. the fragrance was just starting

4. Peeping in the doorway, I saw my mother was laying across the bed, pressing a handkerchief to her mouth.

   Olive Ann Burns, *Cold Sassy Tree*

   4a. was running along the sidewalk

   4b. walking down the road

   4c. holding a package in his hands

   4d. Janine saw a man

5. In the starlight, her eyes saw an owl, two rabbits, a striped cat from town, a jay sleeping on a branch.

   Hal Borland, *When the Legends Die*

   5a. his glance admired a poster

   5b. a dirty uniform from the game

   5c. from his bed

   5d. two soccer cleats

   5e. a trophy sitting on his dresser

ACTIVITY 4: WRITING IMITATIONS

PART ONE

Look closely at the model and a sample imitation, and then write your own imitation.

1. *Model Sentence:* Eragon bowed slightly, delighted.

   Christopher Paolini, *Eragon*

   Sample Imitation: Daddy laughed lightly, pleased.

2. *Model Sentence:* In a few minutes, Sadako was in an examining room where a nurse x-rayed her chest and took some of her blood.

   Eleanor Coerr, *Sadako and the Thousand Paper Cranes*

   Sample Imitation: After a brief wait, the passengers were in a security checkpoint, where a guard examined their identification and asked questions about their status.

3. *Model Sentence:* The wheels struck the runway, and the plane pulled up by a small wooden house, the terminal building.

   Jean Craighead George, *Julie of the Wolves*

   Sample Imitation: The moon revealed the landscape, and the fugitives crouched low beside a dark silent barracks, the prisoners' dormitory.

4. *Model Sentence:* When she passed through the shrubbery gate, she found herself in great gardens, with wide lawns and winding walks with clipped borders.

   Frances Hodgson Burnett, *The Secret Garden*

   Sample Imitation: After they traveled from great distances, they enjoyed themselves within the gorgeous golf course, with sloping hills and narrow creeks with neat banks.

5. *Model Sentence:* Where the woods thinned, Taran clattered along a dry stream bed until, exhausted, he stumbled and held out his hands against the whirling ground.

   Lloyd Alexander, *The Book of Three*

   Sample Imitation: After the waters receded, the land dried within the area until, crusted, it cracked and hardened its surface from the searing heat.

PART TWO

Copy the model sentence and the one sentence that imitates it. Then write your own imitation of the same model about something from your imagination or from a TV show, movie, story, or book. When you finish, you will have three sentences all built the same way—the model sentence, the imitation sentence, and your imitation sentence.

6. *Model:* One of their dogs, the best one, had disappeared.
   Fred Gipson, *Old Yeller*

   a. One of the reasons to save is for money for college.

   b. One of their smallest cars, a subcompact Fiat, was featured.

   c. One of his most valuable baseball cards was missing.

7. *Model:* When I was in elementary school, I packed my suitcase and told my mother I was going to run away from home.
   Jean Craighead George, *My Side of the Mountain*

   a. After we finished the third inning in the play-off game, we led the score and reassured our coach we were going to go the distance to win.

   b. When in doubt, always seek the help of a policeman to find your parents because police are usually very friendly with kids and want to help.

   c. At the end of my senior year, I graduated from high school and told my parents I was going to head immediately for college.

8. *Model:* Standing there in the middle of the street, Marty suddenly thought of Halloween, of the winter and snowballs, of the schoolyard.
   Murray Heyert, "The New Kid"

a. Getting stuff addressed to me in the mail when I was a kid was always a big thrill, and made me feel like a grown-up who had his own mail.

b. Slugs are often found in dark places, under rocks, for example, and they move hardly at all, just sitting there and being very sluggish.

c. Readying for the summer vacation from school, Francisco always anticipated days of sunshine, of the morning mist and evening fireflies, of sweet fruit.

9. *Model:* My mother ran through the winding sidewalks with me in her arms, shrieking, then took me to the hospital where I received five tiny stitches.

Sarah Dessen, *Dreamland*

a. My dentist, who has been in practice for forty years, always greets kids wearing a funny mask with his white coat, and then promises children candy when he's finished.

b. On top of the house, with a loud crack, a tree branch landed, denting the roof in a place that allowed driving rain to enter and flood the family room.

c. Our school bus drove through the traffic jam with caution throughout the route, halting, then drove us to our school where we arrived five minutes late.

10. *Model:* A short, round boy of seven, he took little interest in troublesome things, preferring to remain on good terms with everyone.

Mildred D. Taylor, *Roll of Thunder, Hear My Cry*

A time to remember for always is the first time you get behind ` wheel of a car and go for a spin all by yourself with no
    ·ctor.

le mysterious, superhero in movies, Batman fights crime in
tham City, striving to establish within that city justice for all.

he Olympics, Michael Phelps achieved tremendous honors for
United States swim team by earning a vast number of medals,
nly gold.

TRONGER PARAGRAPHS

ph (<u>ten to fifteen sentences</u>) to create an incident that could
unger Games or *Catching Fire* or *Mockingjay* (or some other
u are familiar with).

[handwritten: autobiographical incident story]

iragraph picturing your imagined incident. Choose *three* of
del sentences to imitate and include them somewhere in
3uild all of your sentences—*not just the three imitations*—
izanne Collins (or the author of your other novel) builds

ES BY SUZANNE COLLINS

ER GAMES

lessly, I turn myself in that direction.

ioon) of my encounter with Peeta Malark, the rain was
sheets.)

ies to dry at the fire, crawl into bed, and fall into a
p.

place I've ever been in, with thick, deep carpets, and a
id chairs.

hunting, my father would whistle or sing complicated
ockingjay birds, and, after a polite pause, the birds
ng back.

FROM CATCHING FIRE

- On the fog comes, silent and steady and flat. ists,
- I sit on the side of my bed, elbows on my kne old
  and watch my glowing suit in the darkness, i
  home in District 12, huddled beside the fire.   rds
- In my stillness, I begin to notice the animal nd
  with brilliant plumage, tree lizards with flic ging
  something that looks like a cross between
  on the branches close to the trunk.
- Taken by surprise and overwhelmed by sh
  keepers were initially overcome by the cr

FROM MOCKINGJAY

- I stare down at my shoes, watching as a   n the
  worn leather.
- I spring up, upsetting a box of a hundr
  scattering around the floor.
- By dawn the bombers were long gon
  stragglers rounded up.
- People keep talking at me, talking,
- Inside is the first beautiful thing I'   rees
  compound, which is a replication
  and flowering plants, and alive wit   in,
- The wounded from this mornings s
  on homemade stretchers, in whe
  shoulders, and clenched tight in
  unconscious.   our

Exchange your draft with other studer s.
paragraph, and also give them sugges

ACTIVITY 2: MATCHING

Match the subjects and their predicates with the tools to make a better sentence with more information. *Write out each sentence, underlining the tools.*

PART ONE

Each tool is a <u>sentence opener</u> because it begins the sentence.

Subjects and Predicates	Tools as Openers
1. ^ , the horse was very lean and bony. Lois Lenski, *Strawberry Girl*	a. Framed by long black locks
2. ^ , the boy's mother would wrap the leftover biscuits in a clean flour sack and put them away for the next meal. William H. Armstrong, *Sounder*	b. Beneath its shaggy coat
3. ^ , he pushed over into a blazing steep dive toward the waves. Richard Bach, *Jonathan Livingston Seagull*	c. From a thousand feet, flapping his wings as hard as he could
4. ^ , we witnessed the sacking of our launch. Pierre Boulle, *Planet of the Apes*	d. Powerless
5. ^ , her deep eyes shone with a driving force. Christopher Paolini, *Eragon*	e. When flour was scarce

PART TWO

Each tool is an <u>S-V split</u> because it comes after the subject and before the verb.

Subjects and Predicates	Tools as S-V Splits
6. Her eyes, ^ , gazed at Kit with longing. Elizabeth George Speare, *The Witch of Blackbird Pond*	**a.** a tan Jersey cow named Blind Tillie
7. Manuel,^ , had been operated on. Hal Borland, *When the Legends Die*	**b.** much too big for her pinched little face
8. One of them, ^ , was Cold Sassy's champion milk producer. Olive Ann Burns, *Cold Sassy Tree*	**c.** who had been sitting, his elbows on his knees, his chin on his fists
9. Laughter, ^ , filled the room. Rosa Guy, *The Friends*	**d.** the herder who shot himself in the foot
10. Mr. Murry, ^ , rose. Madeleine L'Engle, *A Wrinkle in Time*	**e.** loud and warm from their long and intimate relationship

PART THREE

Each tool is a <u>sentence closer</u> because it ends the sentence.

Subjects and Predicates	Tools as Closers
11. Her necklace popped loose, ^ . Lynne Rae Perkins, *Criss Cross*	**a.** a white flash in his headlights, like a large rat
12. The houses were set out in a line under the soft green trees, ^ . Willie Morris, *My Dog Skip*	**b.** their leaves rustling gently with the breeze
13. The dog wagged his tail so hard that he knocked some oranges off the display, ^ . Kate DiCamillo, *Because of Winn-Dixie*	**c.** thirty-six droplets of life so tiny that Eduardo could see them only under a microscope
14. In the beginning there were thirty-six of them, ^ . Nancy Farmer, *The House of the Scorpion*	**d.** flinging itself from her neck onto a bright, fuzzy photograph of a boy and a girl, laughing, having fun against a backdrop of sparkling water
15. Something dashed across the road, ^ . Michael Crichton, *Jurassic Park*	**e.** sending them rolling everywhere, mixing in with the tomatoes and onions and green peppers

PART FOUR

Choose the best place to put each tool—opener, S-V split, or closer.

Subjects and Predicates	Tools
16. I felt a welt and a crust of hardened blood. Avi, *Crispin: The Cross of Lead*	**a.** chin trembling, telling us about the accident on the highway
17. They huddle together. Suzanne Collins, *Catching Fire*	**b.** putting a hand to my forehead
18. Mother temporarily gave up her hairpieces. Jacqueline Kelly, *The Evolution of Calpurnia Tate*	**c.** a crimped false fringe and a rolled horsehair rat, platforms on which she daily constructed an elaborate mountain of her own hair
19. The guitarist on the stage let pure drops of sound fall into the noisy room. Lynne Rae Perkins, *Criss Cross*	**d.** tuning his guitar
20. Momma looked at Poppa's empty chair and waiting plate, then she turned to us. Ingrid Law, *Savvy*	**e.** eating, blowing on their tea, and taking tiny, scalding sips as I build up the fire

ACTIVITY 3: UNSCRAMBLING TO IMITATE

In the models and the scrambled lists of sentence parts, identify subjects, predicates, and tools. Unscramble and write out the sentence parts to imitate the model. Then write your own imitation of the same model, using for content something from your imagination or from a TV show, movie, story, or book.

1. *Model:* She looked up, surprised and flattered.

    Elizabeth George Speare, *The Witch of Blackbird Pond*

    a. sat down

    b. relaxed

    c. Cranston

    d. and relieved

2. *Model:* I could hear Momma and Rocket downstairs, sweeping up glass and replacing light bulbs.

    Ingrid Law, *Savvy*

    a. and pulling its ears

    b. I

    c. playing with their dog

    d. could see Sam and Nate outside

3. *Model:* Framed by long black locks, her deep eyes shone with a driving force.

    Christopher Paolini, *Eragon*

    a. disappeared

    b. covered by dark musty quilts

    c. the valuable paintings

    d. in a hidden room

4. *Model:* The class drifted off to lunch, the girls holding their stomachs, and the guys pushing each other around and acting like doofuses.

Rick Riordan, The Lightning Thief

    a. the animals

    b. and the cats circling their cages and moving like dancers

    c. settled down for a while

    d. the monkeys grooming each other

5. *Model:* On the next try, everything was perfect, even the punctuation.

Roald Dahl, "The Great Grammatizator"

    a. not even the baby

    b. no one

    c. in the early morning

    d. was awake

6. *Model:* If you take a bad boy and make him dig a hole every day in the hot sun, it will turn him into a good boy.

Louis Sachar, Holes

    a. and make him prepare a meal every night in an equipped kitchen

    b. it

    c. if you take a novice cook

    d. may turn him into a fine chef

7. *Model:* He doodled on his desk, drawing contour maps of mountain-ous islands and then telling his desk to display them in three dimensions from every angle.

Orson Scott Card, *Ender's Game*

a. sharing soothing memories of lovely beaches

b. whispered in her ear

c. and then causing her brain to replay those memories in her sleep with every dream

d. he

8. *Model:* Curled up on one of her pillows, a gray fluff of kitten yawned, showing its pink tongue, tucked its head under again, and went back to sleep.

Madeleine L'Engle, *A Wrinkle in Time*

a. stretched

b. sprawled out on one of the chairs

c. flexing his skinny legs

d. a lanky bit of boy

e. planted his feet on the floor, and stood up to walk

9. *Model:* Maybeth was up in her room, doing some of the many extra assignments her teacher gave her, so that she could catch up with the rest of the third graders and not be kept back again.

Cynthia Voigt, *Dicey's Song*

a. was out on the field

b. so that he could stay up with the rest of the team

c. and not be left out anymore

    d. Duncan

    e. running some of the many extra laps the coach gave him

10. *Model:* The leader of the Winged Monkeys flew up to Dorothy, his long, hairy arms stretching out and his ugly face grinning terribly, but he saw the mark of the Good Witch's kiss upon her forehead and stopped short, motioning the others not to touch her.

L. Frank Baum, The Wonderful Wizard of Oz

    a. but it took the piece of the carefully offered meat from his hand

    b. its pointed inquiring snout sniffing him

    c. the scariest of the dog pack

    d. and backed away

    e. came up to Henry

    f. and its menacing growl threatening ominously

    g. signaling the others not to approach him

ACTIVITY 4: COMBINING TO IMITATE

In the models, identify subjects, predicates, and tools. Then, combine the list of sentences to imitate the model. Finally, write your own imitation about something from your imagination or from a TV show, movie, story, or book.

  1. *Model:* He remained unnaturally quiet, a long pale sword in his hand.

Christopher Paolini, Eragon

    a. She appeared.

    b. She appeared beautifully dressed.

    c. She had a bright colorful scarf across her shoulders.

2. *Model:* The class drifted off to lunch, the girls holding their stomachs, the guys pushing each other around and acting like doofuses.

> Rick Riordan, *The Lightning Thief*

   a. The fish darted toward the glass.

   b. The little ones were fluttering their tails.

   c. The big ones were bumping each other sideways and moving in pairs.

3. *Model:* Cupping his hands tightly around his lips, he pitched the call high enough to make it sound like a young turkey gobbling.

> Virginia Hamilton, *M. C. Higgins, the Great*

   a. Jermayne was moving the brush quickly across the paper.

   b. He made the circle red enough to make it look like something.

   c. It looked like a small traffic stoplight.

4. *Model:* All four members of Maxwell, the other team in the final round, were in the eighth grade.

> E. L. Konigsburg, *The View from Saturday*

   a. This is about all amazing elements of magic.

   b. That was the fascinating topic of the guest magician.

   c. All those elements of magic were in the possible realm.

5. *Model:* There were three men, all in dark suits, standing on the front porch.

> Gary Paulsen, *The River*

   a. There were two children.

   b. Both children were in bright colors.

   c. They were playing on the school playground.

6. *Model:* Howard stood in the darkened doorway, cold, wet, and muddy.

     Paul Harding, *Tinkers*

   a. Meagan hid in the dark room.

   b. She was silent.

   c. She was anxious.

   d. Also, she was frightened.

7. *Model:* She noticed two small blackbirds nearby, panting like dogs from the heat, their beaks open, their feathers puffed up.

     Susan Patron, *The Higher Power of Lucky*

   a. Clara watched several crimson balloons overhead.

   b. The balloons were floating like leaves from the trees.

   c. Their bodies were firm.

   d. Their strings were dangling down.

8. *Model:* They threw away their lives for money, for packets of powder, for a stranger's charming smile.

     Cassandra Clare, *City of Bones*

   a. They squandered their talents for several reasons.

   b. They squandered them for pennies.

   c. They squandered them for images of notoriety.

   d. They squandered them for an agent's promise.

   e. The agent's promise was deceptive.

9. *Model:* He raised one eyebrow, stared at me for five seconds, then stomped to the recliner and sat down on the very edge, his back ramrod straight.

     Stephenie Meyer, *Breaking Dawn*

   a. She lifted the envelope.

   b. She ripped it open in one movement.

   c. She then looked at the letter.

   d. And she read through to the end.

   e. Her tears were welling up.

10. *Model:* In the quiet, I heard them beyond the corral, Cyclone barking, and the lamb making its kind of noise, and the ewe making her kind of noise.

     Joseph Krumgold, . . . *And Now Miguel*

   a. This happened at the pharmacy.

   b. What happened was I saw the parents between the aisles.

   c. Henry was loitering.

   d. And his wife was thumbing through a magazine.

   e. And their child was crawling around beneath them.

REVIEW

There are three kinds of sentence parts: *subjects*, *predicates*, and *tools*. Tools add detail and dazzle to sentences.

TOOL FACTS

1. Tools are removable sentence parts. If you can remove it without destroying the rest of the sentence, it's a tool. If you cannot remove it without destroying the rest of the sentence, it is not a tool.

2. Tools can be included in a sentence at the beginning, in the middle, or at the end. Tools at the beginning are called *openers*; tools between the subject and its verb are called *S-V splits*; tools at the end are called *closers*.

TOOL (*removable*)

I was sitting in a baby carrier on the floor, **strapped in and safe as I checked out my world of green shag carpet and matching sofa.**

NOT A TOOL (*nonremovable*)

I was sitting in a baby carrier on the floor, strapped in and safe as I checked out my world of green shag carpet and matching sofa.

Sharon M. Draper, *Out of My Mind*

OPENER (*comma after the tool*)

When the anthem finished and the screen went dark, a hush fell on the room.

Suzanne Collins, *The Hunger Games*

S-V SPLIT (*comma before and after the tool*)

Two boys, **each carrying a shovel,** were coming across the compound.

Louis Sachar, *Holes*

CLOSER (*comma before the tool*)

The necklace I have always wanted now weighs me down, **a shiny, hateful thing.**

Libba Bray, *A Great and Terrible Beauty*

3. A tool can be a word.

WORD

Overhead, swallows flitted, free as birds ever are.

Avi, *Crispin: The Cross of Lead*

4. A tool can be a phrase. *Phrases* are groups of words that don't contain a subject and predicate.

PHRASE

Brown, **the wife of an American diplomat at the U.S. embassy in Amman**, coached volleyball.

Warren St. John, *Outcasts United*

5. A tool can be a dependent clause. Clauses are groups of words that contain a subject and predicate. A dependent clause is a sentence part attached to a complete sentence.

CLAUSE (*dependent*)

My sister turned from the river and closed her eyes, **as though she could wish away the river**.

Fanny Billingsley, *Chime*

6. Sentences can have more than one tool of the same kind. These are called *multiples*.

MULTIPLE TOOLS

A shaft of sunlight, **warm** and **thin**, lay across his body. (*words*)

Marjorie Kinnan Rawlings, *The Yearling*

She noticed two small blackbirds nearby, **their beaks open, their feathers puffed up.** (*phrases*)

Susan Patron, *The Higher Power of Lucky*

That face belonged to Phoebe Winterbottom, **who had a powerful imagination, who would become my friend, and who would have many peculiar things happen to her.** (*clauses*)

Sharon Creech, *Walk Two Moons*

7. Sentences can have a combination of different tools called *combos*. They can be together or apart.	**COMBO TOOLS** *Together:* The only light in here came from the fireplace, **where a bright blaze of logs settled slightly** (*clause*), **sending a fountain of sparks up into the chimney** (*phrase*). Philip Pullman, *The Golden Compass* *Apart:* **Slowly** (*word*), she turned back to Simon, **knowing how she must look to him, standing alone in a damp storage room, her feet tangled in bright plastic wiring cables** (*phrases*). Cassandra Clare, *City of Bones*
8. Tools can be short, medium, or long.	**SHORT** (*1–5 words*) Two boys, **each carrying a shovel**, were coming across the compound. Louis Sachar, *Holes* **MEDIUM** (*6–10 words*) **When I was four and Cass was six,** she whacked me across the face with a plastic shovel at our neighborhood park. Sarah Dessen, *Dreamland* **LONG** (*10+ words*) By the door lay another dog, **its brown eyes open and watchful in contrast to the peacefulness radiated by the other occupants of the room.** Sheila Burnford, *The Incredible Journey*

BUILDING STRONGER PARAGRAPHS

Authors pepper their sentences with tools to increase interest, content, and style. In the following paragraph, a character in Michael Crichton's *Jurassic Park* has fallen into a leech-infested swamp and discovers, to his horror, a blood-sucking leech clinging to his lip.

Contrast the following two versions of the paragraph, the first without tools and the second (the original) with tools. The author uses all three kinds of tools: word, phrase, clause. In the original paragraph with tools, notice their power.

WITHOUT TOOLS

(1) The side of his mouth felt funny. (2) He touched his face and felt swollen flesh. (3) He realized the swollen flesh was a leech. (4) It was practically in his mouth. (5) He pulled the leech away. (6) He spat, and flung it. (7) He saw another leech on his forearm, and pulled it off.

WITH TOOLS

The Leech

(1) The side of his mouth felt funny, **numb** and **tingling**.
(2) **Wondering if he had hurt it during the fall,** he touched his face, and, **on the side of his mouth,** felt swollen flesh. (3) **Suddenly,** he realized the swollen flesh was a leech, **growing fat as it sucked his lips**. (4) It was practically in his mouth. (5) **Shivering with nausea,** he pulled the leech away, **feeling it tear from the flesh of his lips, feeling the gush of warm blood in his mouth**. (6) He spat, and flung it **with disgust into the forest**. (7) He saw another leech on his forearm, and pulled it off, **which left a dark bloody streak behind.**

Words	*numb, tingling, suddenly*
Phrases	*wondering if he had hurt it during the fall,* *on the side of his mouth,* *growing fat as it sucked his lips,* *shivering with nausea,* *feeling it tear from the flesh of his lips* *feeling the gush of warm blood in his mouth* *with disgust into the forest*
Clause	*which left a dark bloody streak behind*

Now it's your turn. The following paragraph is based upon an incident in Stephen King's story "The Body" in which a group of middle school boys, camped out in a forest at night, are awakened and startled by a loud, terrifying sound. In the version that follows, Stephen King's tools have been removed.

At each caret mark (^), add a tool to make the paragraph even more terrifying. For the tools you add, choose what works best—a word, a phrase, or a dependent clause. Use all three at least once.

The Scream

(1) A long, loud, and hollow scream rose from the woods, ^ .
(2) The wild, sobbing cry rose into the night again, ^ , ^ . (3) The scream climbed with a crazy ease through octave after octave, ^ .
(4) It hung there for a moment and then whirled back down again, ^ . (5) This was followed by a burst of what sounded like mad laughter, and then there was silence again. **[ADD ANYWHERE TWO MORE SPECTACULAR, SCARY SENTENCES WITH LOTS OF SENTENCE-COMPOSING TOOLS!]**

REVIEW

Words, phrases, and clauses are the tools that build better sentences and paragraphs by adding detail and dazzle.

PREVIEW

Authors use those tools in three places within their sentences. You'll learn those three places to use tools to build good sentences, and through them, better paragraphs, using this worktext as your owner's manual.

TOOL PLACES

Authors vary where they put tools, those important sentence parts that add dazzle and detail to sentences. Those tools—whether words, phrases, or dependent clauses—can be moved around within sentences, just like furniture in your room.

Your bed in your room isn't nailed to the floor, right? Well, neither are most words, phrases, and dependent clauses glued to just one place in a sentence. Just as you can move your bed around the room to find a better place, authors can move sentence parts within a sentence to place them effectively.

With sentences, you have three choices for placing sentence parts: *opener, S-V split, closer*.

Good writers use all three places. You can, too. Next, you'll learn and practice how they do it. It's a good thing to know how to move things around to put them in better places, including sentence parts.

For me the big chore is always the same: how to begin a sentence, how to continue it, how to complete it.

—Claude Simon, *winner of the Nobel Prize in literature*

THE OPENER

Sometimes, authors use tools at the front of the sentence to provide information immediately because it's important. Take a look at sentences without tools up front. There's not much detail or dazzle in those sentences. Then compare them to sentences with tools up front called *openers* because they come at the opening of the sentence.

1a. I went to sleep again.

1b. <u>After a bit</u>, <u>lulled by the bobbing of the raft and by the soft</u>, <u>pleasant sounds of the sea against the oil barrel floats</u>, I went to sleep again.

Theodore Taylor, *The Cay*

2a. He began to wonder if he should give up and go home.

2b. <u>About midnight</u>, <u>huddled shivering under his blankets in the darkness</u>, he began to wonder if he should give up and go home.

Thomas Rockwell, *How to Eat Fried Worms*

3a. He sat on the grass.

3b. <u>Awkwardly</u>, <u>with his legs angled out in front of him</u>, he sat on the grass.

Betsy Byars, *The Summer of the Swans*

4a. Things started to get easier.

4b. <u>After the initial few weeks of school</u>, <u>when everything seemed gloomy and I still brooded a great deal about having left home</u>, things started to get easier.

Ved Mehta, "A Donkey in a World of Horses"

5a. You would be prepared for any sort of remarkable tale.

5b. <u>Truly, if you had heard only a quarter of what I have heard about Gandalf,</u> you would be prepared for any sort of remarkable tale.

J. R. R. Tolkien, The Hobbit

An opener is any tool at the beginning of a sentence. Openers can be *words*, *phrases*, or *clauses*. Below are examples from the above sentences.

WORDS

- awkwardly
- truly

PHRASES

- after a bit
- lulled by the bobbing of the raft and by the soft, pleasant sounds of the sea against the oil barrel floats
- about midnight
- huddled shivering under his blankets in the darkness
- with his legs angled out in front of him
- after the initial few weeks of school

CLAUSES

- when everything seemed gloomy and I still brooded a great deal about having left home

- if you had heard only a quarter of what I have heard about Gandalf

ACTIVITY 1: MATCHING

Match the opener with its sentence. Write out each sentence, inserting the opener at the caret mark (^) and underlining it. Name the kind of opener—*word*, *phrase*, or *clause*. **Punctuation:** Use a comma after each opener.

Sentence	Opener
1. ^ , the gods will grant her wish and make her healthy again. Eleanor Coerr, *Sadako and the Thousand Paper Cranes*	**a.** the size of a five-year-old girl
2. ^ , the men of Soror were upon us before we could lift our weapons to our shoulders. Pierre Boulle, *Planet of the Apes*	**b.** hungry
3. ^ , Grant saw an island, rugged and craggy, rising sharply from the ocean. Michael Crichton, *Jurassic Park*	**c.** if a sick person folds one thousand paper cranes
4. ^ , she was even more exquisite than the doll he'd made for the infant Empress. Maggie Stiefvater, *Forever*	**d.** leaping out of the thickets like stags
5. ^ , Thomas ate two portions of meat. Hal Borland, *When the Legends Die*	**d.** ahead

ACTIVITY 2: COMBINING

Combine each pair of sentences by making the underlined part an opener for the other sentence. The result is the sentence the author wrote—one sentence instead of two to say the same thing! Don't forget the comma after the opener.

EXAMPLE

Two Sentences

He pitched the call high enough to make it sound like a young turkey gobbling. He did this while <u>cupping his hands tightly around his lips</u>.

One Sentence with Opener

<u>Cupping his hands tightly around his lips</u>, he pitched the call high enough to make it sound like a young turkey gobbling.

Virginia Hamilton, *M. C. Higgins, the Great*

WORDS

1. I felt the fur at the back of my neck prickle and rise. I felt <u>uneasy</u>.
   Maggie Stiefvater, *Forever*

2. He released the tension from his bow and moved forward. He did this <u>cautiously</u>.

   Christopher Paolini, *Eragon*

3. The clouds were thick and dark, giving warning that this is monsoon season, when floods of rain could fall from the sky in a matter of minutes. The clouds were <u>overhead</u>.

    Libba Bray, *A Great and Terrible Beauty*

4. He really felt as if the whole car were moving beneath him. He was <u>dizzy and nauseous</u>.

    Michael Crichton, *Jurassic Park*

5. He wandered about the many tents, only to find that one place was as cold as another. He was <u>miserable and disconsolate</u>.

    Jack London, *The Call of the Wild*

PHRASES

6. Warriors on high stilts beat upraised swords against their shields. This happened <u>around the fiery circle</u>.

    Lloyd Alexander, *The Book of Three*

7. I went to sleep again. I had been <u>lulled by the bobbing of the raft and by the soft</u>, <u>pleasant sounds of the sea against the oil barrel floats</u>.

    Theodore Taylor, *The Cay*

8. The wolves trotted away. The wolves were <u>drooping their tails and glancing warily at her</u>.

    Jean Craighead George, *Julie of the Wolves*

9. Spencer V. Silverthorne, a young buyer for Nuget's department store, slumbered. Spender was <u>buried in a nearby leather armchair</u>.

    Walter Lord, *A Night to Remember*

10. On the floor lay an old white English bull terrier. The terrier had <u>his scarred</u>, <u>bony head resting on one of the man's feet</u>.

    Sheila Burnford, *The Incredible Journey*

CLAUSES

11. A fuzzy spider paced across the room. This happened <u>while she sat there</u>.

    Eleanor Coerr, *Sadako and the Thousand Paper Cranes*

12. Angus Phail died. He died <u>before little Ramona was a year old</u>.

    Helen Hunt Jackson, *Ramona*

13. His wife came to meet him at the door. She did this <u>as he drew near to the cottage</u>.

    Daphne du Maurier, "The Birds"

14. We were let out into the playground twice a day for a short recess and at lunchtime. This occurred <u>if the weather cooperated</u>.

    Keith Donohue, *The Stolen Child*

15. Cass whacked me across the face with a plastic shovel at our neighborhood park. This happened <u>when I was four and when Cass was six</u>.

    Sarah Dessen, *Dreamland*

ACTIVITY 3: UNSCRAMBLING

Unscramble both lists of sentence parts to imitate the same model. Write out each imitation sentence, underline its opener, and tell the types: *word*, *phrase*, or *clause*. **Note:** *Some sentences have more than one opener.*

EXAMPLE

Model to Imitate: Looking into the inside of the wardrobe, she saw several coats hanging up, mostly fur coats.

C. S. Lewis, *The Chronicles of Narnia*

List One	List Two
a. the rat	**a.** obviously concerned fans
b. mainly wild mongrels	**b.** spotted people jumping up
c. observed dogs running fast	**c.** falling down near the home plate
d. peering around the garbage can	**d.** the runner
Imitation: <u>Peering around the garbage can</u>, the rat observed dogs running fast, mainly wild mongrels. (*phrase*)	**Imitation:** <u>Falling down near the home plate</u>, the runner spotted people jumping up, obviously concerned fans. (*phrase*)

First Model: When the hole got too deep for our shovels to reach bottom, I climbed down into it.

Hillary Jordan, *Mudbound*

1a. looked into easier steps	**2a.** Mom
1b. the instructor	**2b.** before the recipe became too advanced for us kids to understand
1c. if the routine got too complicated for the beginning dancers to follow	**2c.** demonstrated the procedure

Second Model: Now, swaggering back, they jeered at the other kids.

Betty Smith, *A Tree Grows in Brooklyn*

3a. looking around	4a. swerved around the dog
3b. then	4b. ahead
3c. walked near the students' desks	4c. the car
3d. the teacher	4d. braking fast

Third Model: Booted and muffled, they clumped out through the sprawling kitchen.

Susan Cooper, *The Dark Is Rising*

5a. the package	6a. but exhausted
5b. and decorated	6b. broke triumphantly through the red ribbon
5c. stayed expectantly on the closet shelf	6c. the winner
5d. wrapped	6d. exhilarated

Fourth Model: Dirty, stinking of sweat and horses, he cradled
the boy against his chest, sat in his wife's old rocker, and closed his eyes.

Kristin Cashore, *Fire*

7a. searching for food and warmth	**8a.** and demonstrated his gizmo
7b. and marked her path	**8b.** uptight
7c. she followed her instincts through the forest	**8c.** walked into the stuffy antique boardroom
7d. alone	**8d.** he held his invention in his arms
7e. looked for some edible nonpoisonous plants	**8e.** worrying about presentation and audience

Fifth Model: In the land of Ingary, where such things as cloaks
of invisibility really exist, it is quite a misfortune to be born the
eldest of three.

Diana Wynne Jones, *Howl's Moving Castle*

9a. to be harvesting a crop	**10a.** in the science of genetics
9b. where extra plants like clumps of weeds sometimes grow	**10b.** where such things as strings of DNA are studied
9c. within the meadow of lavender	**10c.** to be chosen the winner
9d. it is always a pleasure	**10d.** it is certainly an honor
9e. in abundance	**10e.** of the fair

ACTIVITY 4: IMITATING

Each model has more than one opener. Match the imitation with its model sentence. Then write your own imitation of the entire model—not just the openers—about something from your imagination or from a TV show, movie, story, or book.

MODEL SENTENCES

1. Fastening the chain back around her neck, trying to tell by feel whether the catch had closed, she thought of another loophole.

   Lynne Rae Perkins, *Criss Cross*

2. Beside the entrance way, looking at her with dark, unblinking eyes, stood the biggest rat she had ever seen.

   Robert C. O'Brien, *Mrs. Frisby and the Rats of NIMH*

3. Tugging the handcart, a home-made contraption with a bar joining its shafts, he and James made their way down the curve.

   Susan Cooper, *The Dark Is Rising*

4. For just an instant, listening to the absolute confidence in his voice, I experienced a rare moment of insight.

   Stephenie Meyer, *Breaking Dawn*

5. On the calmest days, when the wind scarcely swayed the smoke from the oven chimney, I saw big white clouds slowly rising above the top of the bakery.

   Pierre Gascar, "The Little Square"

IMITATIONS

A. In under a minute, moving with the skilled intensity of a champion, the skater completed the difficult sequence of moves.

B. Dragging the rug back up the stairs, hoping to reach the top where the room was located, he pulled with Herculean strength.

C. On the skyline, standing with its solid, unmovable height, loomed the tallest building the city had ever built.

D. In the best moments, when my heart gently sang the song of our lasting love, I felt many special memories gently emanating from the warmth of your smile.

E. Singing the tune, a Broadway melody with a refrain echoing its theme, he and I kept our spirits from great sadness.

ACTIVITY 5: EXCHANGING

If the opener is a *word*, exchange it for a new word. If the opener is a *phrase*, exchange it for a new phrase. If the opener is a *dependent clause*, exchange it for a new dependent clause. Write out the complete sentence. **Note:** *Some sentences have more than one opener.*

EXAMPLE: WORD OPENER

Original Sentence: **Silently**, we slipped into the brush and fell flat to the ground.

Mildred D. Taylor, *Roll of Thunder, Hear My Cry*

Sample Exchanges

- **Suddenly,** we slipped into the brush and fell flat to the ground.

- **Quickly,** we slipped into the brush and fell flat to the ground.

- **Luckily,** we slipped into the brush and fell flat to the ground.

-----

1. **Discouraged,** she wriggled backward down the frost heave and arrived at her camp feet first.

     Jean Craighead George, *Julie of the Wolves*

2. **Ahead,** sharp red clusters of taillights traced a broken line down the dropping twists of the divided highway.

     Carl Henry Rathjen, "Runaway Rig"

3. **Excited,** he lifted a thin lip in a snarl.

     Christopher Paolini, *Eragon*

4. **Quickly** and **noisily,** Gerard came in.

     Elizabeth Bowen, "Foothold"

5. **Then, dented, scratched,** and **steaming,** the car rumbled off into the darkness, its rear lights blazing angrily.

     J. K. Rowling, *Harry Potter and the Chamber of Secrets*

EXAMPLE: PHRASE OPENER

Original Sentence: **To qualify for the racing team in junior high,** she would have to practice every day.

     Eleanor Coerr, *Sadako and the Thousand Paper Cranes*

Sample Exchanges

- **To try to regain her strength in her legs,** she would have to practice every day.

- **To prove that she could maintain self-discipline,** she would have to practice every day.

- **To qualify for the first round of the tryouts,** she would have to practice every day.

---

6. **A short, round boy of seven,** he took little interest in troublesome things, preferring to remain on good terms with everyone.
   Mildred D. Taylor, *Roll of Thunder, Hear My Cry*

7. **Her heart hammering in her chest,** Clary ducked behind the nearest concrete pillar and peered around it.
   Cassandra Clare, *City of Bones*

8. **Calling to each other, hooting like owls loose in the daytime,** we worked all morning in opposite parts of the woods.
   Truman Capote, *The Grass Harp*

9. **Outside the window, in the blue moonlight,** she could see a huge jagged slab of ice sticking up from the snow.
   Susan Fromberg Schaeffer, *Time in Its Flight*

10. **Coming down the street, towering over everyone like some giant in a fairy story, showing off his well-tailored gray suit with its diamond tiepin glittering in the sun,** strode Calvin.
    Rosa Guy, *The Friends*

EXAMPLE: CLAUSE OPENER

Original Sentence: **After a rock hit Billy over the eye**, he sat down backward in the mud, covering his head with his arms, sobbing.

Thomas Rockwell, *How to Eat Fried Worms*

Sample Exchanges

- **While he thought about what happened at school that day**, he sat down backward in the mud, covering his head with his arms, sobbing.

- **When the bully called him a freak**, he sat down backward in the mud, covering his head with his arms, sobbing.

- **Although he was dressed in his new expensive jeans and his favorite designer T-shirt**, he sat down backward in the mud, covering his head with his arms, sobbing.

---

11. **When she was a sickly, fretful, ugly little baby**, she was kept out of the way.

     Frances Hodgson Burnett, *The Secret Garden*

12. **After Uncle Daniels had finished with his lamb-chop dinner**, I set the cream puffs on the coffee table and stood back looking at them.

     Rosa Guy, *Edith Jackson*

13. **When the tinkling little melody began**, Winnie's sobbing slowed.

     Natalie Babbitt, *Tuck Everlasting*

5a. Anne Frank wrote without reserve about her likes and dislikes.

5b. Anne Frank, <u>who was thirteen when she began her diary and fifteen when she was forced to stop</u>, wrote without reserve about her likes and dislikes.

Otto H. Frank and Mirjam Pressler (editors),
The Diary of Anne Frank

An S-V split is any tool between a subject and its verb. S-V splits can be *words*, *phrases*, or *clauses*. Below are examples from the above sentences.

WORDS

- *smeared*
- *blotted*

PHRASES

- *gasping for breath*
- *his face tear-streaked*
- *clutching his wrist*

CLAUSES

- *because it was closest to the garbage in the empty lot*
- *who was thirteen when she began her diary and fifteen when she was forced to stop*

ACTIVITY 1: MATCHING

Match the S-V split with its sentence. Write out each sentence, inserting the S-V split at the caret mark (^) and underlining it. Name the kind of S-V split—*word*, *phrase*, or *dependent clause*. **Punctuation:** Use a comma before and after each S-V split.

Sentence	S-V Split
1. At one point a raven, ^ , came flapping out from a bush and flew alongside us. Bill and Vera Cleaver, *Where the Lilies Bloom*	**a.** who would not take advantage of a man born without arms or legs or eyes
2. Strangely, people of honest feelings and sensibility, ^ , think nothing of abusing a man born with low intelligence. Daniel Keyes, "Flowers for Algernon"	**b.** his charred clothes fuming where the blast had blown out the fire
3. His paper, ^ , made Grant a celebrity overnight. Michael Crichton, *Jurassic Park*	**c.** black and lustrous
4. The Earl of Mackworth, ^ , kept a small army of Knights. Howard Pyle, *Men of Iron*	**d.** with its report of a herd of ten thousand duck-billed dinosaurs living along the shore of a vast inland sea, building communal nests of eggs in the mud, raising their infant dinosaurs in the herd
5. A seared man, ^ , rose from the curb. Fritz Leiber, "A Bad Day for Sales"	**e.** like other lords

ACTIVITY 2: COMBINING

Combine each pair of sentences by making the underlined part an S-V split for the other sentence. The result is the sentence the author wrote—one sentence instead of two to say the same thing! Don't forget the commas before and after the S-V split.

EXAMPLE

Two Sentences

The thermometer on the patio did climb to over a hundred degrees.

The thermometer was <u>hanging there in the direct sun</u>.

One Sentence with S-V Split

The thermometer on the patio, <u>hanging there in the direct sun</u>, did climb to over a hundred degrees.

Edward Bloor, *Tangerine*

WORDS

1. A woman of fifty or so with frizzy gray hair came toward them down the dark hall. She was <u>plump</u>.
   Katherine Paterson, *Park's Quest*

2. In the moonlight, these three trains confirmed my fears that traffic was not maintained by night on this part of the line. The trains were <u>motionless</u>.
   Winston Churchill, "I Escape from the Boers"

3. Spitz left the pack and cut across a narrow neck of land where the creek made a long bend around. Spitz was <u>cold and calculating</u>.

    Jack London, *The Call of the Wild*

4. The Sunday clothing of the two shoeless boys hung loosely upon their frail frames. Their clothing was <u>patched and worn</u>.

    Mildred D. Taylor, *Roll of Thunder, Hear My Cry*

5. Every year, this aged old hat sorted new students into the four Hogwarts houses. The hat was <u>patched</u>, <u>frayed</u>, <u>and dirty</u>.

    J. K. Rowling, *Harry Potter and the Chamber of Secrets*

PHRASES

6. Anna turned to face me and nodded slightly. Anna was <u>one of my best friends</u>.

    Melina Marchetta, *Looking for Alibrandi*

7. Two boys were coming across the compound. The boys were <u>each carrying a shovel</u>.

    Louis Sachar, *Holes*

8. The boy picked out a blurred shape in the dark. The boy had been <u>trained in night-sight when the lantern was dimmed so as not to alert the wood's creatures</u>.

    William H. Armstrong, *Sounder*

9. The meat hung in the smoke-house. The meat had been <u>dry-cured for the feeding of the dogs</u>.

    Marjorie Kinnan Rawlings, *The Yearling*

10. Lockhart was waving for silence. He was <u>wearing lurid pink robes to match the decorations</u>.

    J. K. Rowling, *Harry Potter and the Chamber of Secrets*

CLAUSES

11. The truck drivers were furious. Their furor happened <u>when they heard that Maxie Hammerman had been released from prison</u>.

    Jean Merrill, *The Pushcart War*

12. The bricks of the chimney provided a point of reference for the rest of the house. Those were the bricks <u>which had collapsed in a charred heap</u>.

    Suzanne Collins, *Mockingjay*

13. George had a little mental handicap radio in his ear. This happened <u>although his intelligence was above normal</u>.

    Kurt Vonnegut, Jr., "Harrison Bergeron"

14. Little Jon should have seen the hole, but all his attention was on the stars. It was Little Jon <u>whose eyes were quicker than most</u>.

    Alexander Key, *The Forgotten Door*

15. The confused man thought for a moment. This was a man <u>who had never liked the words "booby" and "booby-hatch" and who liked them even less on a shining morning when there was a unicorn in the garden</u>.

    James Thurber, "The Unicorn in the Garden"

ACTIVITY 3: UNSCRAMBLING

Unscramble both lists of sentence parts to imitate the same model. Write out each imitation sentence, underline its S-V split, and tell the type: *word*, *phrase*, or *clause*.

EXAMPLE

Model to Imitate: The children, screaming, came charging back into their homeroom.

Rosa Guy, *The Friends*

List One	List Two
a. mewing	**a.** began celebrating loudly on the street
b. were snuggling up against their warm mother	**b.** many fans
c. three kittens	**c.** dancing
Imitation: Three kittens, <u>mewing</u>, were snuggling up against their warm mother. (*word S-V split*)	**Imitation:** Many fans, <u>dancing</u>, began celebrating loudly on the street. (*word S-V split*)

First Model: Fred Stewart, a thin, wiry little man with sunken cheeks and bloodshot eyes, met them.

Laurence E. Stotz, "Fire"

1a. a stately, tall older woman	**2a.** a pudgy, cute little boy
1b. watched them	**2b.** Nate Wilkinson
1c. with chiseled features and striking eyes	**2c.** hugged the puppy
1d. Selma Brooks	**2d.** with curly hair and a huge grin

4. Romey's fried ham and Devola's biscuits, slathered thick with real butter and sourwood honey, sustained us.

   Bill and Vera Cleaver, *Where the Lilies Bloom*

5. The stocky, broad-shouldered man in the doorman's uniform, standing with feet spread, fists on hips, was Sandy McSouthers.

   Ellen Raskin, *The Westing Game*

IMITATIONS

A. Underneath, the hidden chest, which completely contained the buried treasure, lasted for centuries.

B. The adorable, freckle-faced girl in the polka-dot dress, giggling with cheeks dimpled, eyes on Tim, was Sarah Southerby.

C. Hardly a single drop, with some dirt in it, lasted.

D. Two very short, stout senior citizens, turning their backs toward the driving rain, were Leo Laskins and Harry Higgins.

E. Frank's roasted potatoes and Judy's salmon, covered over with ginger jam and squeezed lemon, tempted us.

ACTIVITY 5: EXCHANGING

If the S-V split is a *word*, exchange it for a new word. If the S-V split is a *phrase*, exchange it for a new phrase. If the S-V split is a *dependent clause*, exchange it for a new dependent clause. Write out the complete sentence.

Note: *Single words rarely occur as S-V splits but do occur as multiples—two or three words—as in the sentences that follow.*

EXAMPLE: WORD S-V SPLIT

Original Sentence: A shaft of sunlight, **warm** and **thin**, like a light patchwork quilt, lay across his body.

Marjorie Kinnan Rawlings, *The Yearling*

Sample Exchanges

* A shaft of sunlight, **golden** and **lovely**, like a light patchwork quilt, lay across his body.

* A shaft of sunlight, **sudden** and **delightful**, like a light patchwork quilt, lay across his body.

* A shaft of sunlight, **dappled** and **dancing**, like a light patchwork quilt, lay across his body.

---

1. Milk on her dress, **sticky** and **sour**, attracted every small flying thing from gnats to grasshoppers.
   Toni Morrison, *Beloved*

2. Old Man Matthews, **gray** and **stocky**, came first, with his two sons, Orion, the elder, and Cling, who was Eugie's age.
   Gina Berriault, "The Stone Boy"

3. Footsteps, **dainty** and **thin**, came along the hall, and a kind-faced lady of some forty years peered at them.
   Ray Bradbury, *The Martian Chronicles*

4. The head of the filing department, **neat**, **quiet**, **attentive**, stood in front of the old man's desk.
   James Thurber, "The Catbird Seat"

5. The wounded rooster, **mortified** and **angered**, **vengeful**, flew up on to her head and in fury clawed her hair.

   Bill and Vera Cleaver, *Where the Lilies Bloom*

EXAMPLE: PHRASE S-V SPLIT

Original Sentence: Dad, **sitting on the edge of the porch,** leaned forward so he could see.

   Elizabeth Coatsworth, "The Story of Wang Li"

Sample Exchanges

- Dad, **hearing the fans burst into applause,** leaned forward so he could see.

- Dad, **moving carefully by shifting his body,** leaned forward so he could see.

- Dad, **standing on his tip toes for a better view,** leaned forward so he could see.

----

6. Captain Eaton, **in his good blue coat**, was shouting orders from the quarterdeck.

   Elizabeth George Speare, *The Witch of Blackbird Pond*

7. The guitarist on the stage, **tuning his guitar**, let pure drops of sound fall into the noisy room.

   Lynne Rae Perkins, *Criss Cross*

8. Calvin, **his face screwed up with grim determination**, did not relax his hold.

   Madeleine L'Engle, *A Wrinkle in Time*

9. Hammond, **to avoid nipped fingers**, discouraged people from petting the elephant.

   Michael Crichton, *Jurassic Park*

10. Gabriel, **wrapped in his inadequate blanket**, was hunched, shivering, and silent.

    Lois Lowry, *The Giver*

EXAMPLE: DEPENDENT CLAUSE S-V SPLIT

Original Sentence: The sound of your voice, **when you are alone**, can be either scary or reassuring.

Stephen King, *Bag of Bones*

Sample Exchanges

- The sound of your voice, **when you try singing**, can be either scary or reassuring.

- The sound of your voice, **after it has been recorded**, can be either scary or reassuring.

- The sound of your voice, **while you cheer for the home team**, can be either scary or reassuring.

----

11. His face, **which was brown and covered with wrinkles**, looked very wise, very ugly, and very kind.

    C. S. Lewis, *The Chronicles of Narnia*

12. The old woman beside him, **whose arm he held**, was hunched over as she shuffled along in her soft slippers.

    Lois Lowry, *The Giver*

13. Violet, **who usually moved slowly in the mornings**, nodded and immediately got out of bed and went to the cardboard box to find some proper clothing.

    Lemony Snicket, *A Series of Unfortunate Events*

14. The porch light, **when I came up the hill from the stable**, did not cheer me.

    Wallace Stegner, *Crossing to Safety*

15. The lowest step, **where the stream collected before it tumbled down a hundred feet and disappeared into the rubbly desert**, was a little platform of stone and sand.

    John Steinbeck, *The Pearl*

ACTIVITY 6: EXPANDING

As you've seen, there's more than one way to add an S-V split to a sentence. For each sentence add a word, then a phrase, then a dependent clause.

- -

EXAMPLE

Reduced Sentence: The sheep, ^ , turned now to stare at him.

WORD: The sheep, <u>startled</u>, turned now to stare at him.

PHRASE: The sheep, <u>a herd of twenty or so</u>, turned now to stare at him.

CLAUSE: The sheep, <u>which had just been unloaded from the transport truck from the farm</u>, turned now to stare at him.

Original Sentence: The sheep, **who had moved lightly away as he had come into the pasture**, turned now to stare at him.
(The S-V split is a dependent clause.)

Katherine Paterson, *Park's Quest*

----

1. One of the dogs, ^ , had disappeared.
   Fred Gipson, *Old Yeller*

2. Sandy and Dennis, ^ , were disgusted.
   Madeleine L'Engle, *A Wrinkle in Time*

3. The canoe, ^ , twisted and shifted in the rushing waters.
   Armstrong Sperry, *Call It Courage*

4. Then the great spider, ^ , came from behind him and came at him.
   J. R. R. Tolkien, *The Hobbit*

5. Mrs. Rachel, ^ , took mental note of everything that was on that table.
   L. M. Montgomery, *Anne of Green Gables*

6. One of the rocks, ^ , jutted out of the water almost at the boat's side.
   Franklin W. Dixon, *The Hardy Boys: The House on the Cliff*

7. Carson Drew, ^ , looked at his daughter.
   Carolyn Keene, *Nancy Drew: The Bungalow Mystery*

8. Sometimes in the night, the ranch people, ^ , heard a roar of hoofs go by.

    John Steinbeck, *The Red Pony*

9. Her face, ^ , was round and thick, and her eyes were like two immense eggs stuck into a white mess of bread dough.

    Ray Bradbury, *The Martian Chronicles*

10. Niss Nedra, ^ , was giving the instructions, and Arlene White, ^ , was acting as demonstrator. [**Note:** This is two sentences joined by *and* with an S-V split in each.]

    Lois Duncan, *A Gift of Magic*

BUILDING STRONGER PARAGRAPHS

Partner with one of the authors that follow to write a descriptive paragraph. Each author's sentence contains an S-V split. Select one of them to include as one sentence in a creative paragraph you write describing the topic given for that sentence. Place the author's sentence anywhere it fits best—the beginning of your paragraph, the end, or somewhere in between.

Author's Sentences: Choose one for your paragraph, and then use your imagination and creativity for the rest of the sentences of your paragraph.

1. TOPIC: *a beautiful scene in nature*

    The water, so clear beneath her that she could see the colors of underwater rocks and the floating fingers of seaweed out afar, rippled under the breeze into a blue field that struck gold from the sun, rippling gold as it moved.

    Cynthia Voigt, *Tree by Leaf*

2. TOPIC: a fantasy with strange creatures

   The creatures, <u>some sitting on chairs</u>, <u>others reclining on a sofa</u>, were all watching him intently.

   > Roald Dahl, *James and the Giant Peach*

3. TOPIC: *a quirky but likeable man*

   He wore an old hat, and a thick scarf, <u>its ends tucked into his coat</u>, was crossed over his chest.

   > Leslie Morris, "Three Shots for Charlie Beston"

4. TOPIC: *a room in an ancient castle*

   The small dragon, <u>eyes closed</u>, wrapped its tail around the bedpost contentedly.

   > Christopher Paolini, *Eragon*

5. TOPIC: *a terrifying incident*

   When the snake reared its evil head and sounded its hair-raising warning, Ima Dean screamed and Romey, <u>who had brought along Roy Luther's gun</u>, blew its head off.

   > Bill and Vera Cleaver, *Where the Lilies Bloom*

In your paragraph's sentences use some openers and some S-V splits, and both in at least one sentence. Create sentences that, in style and content, match the style and content of the author's sentence—so good that the author would be proud to have you as a partner.

Your Paragraph: Plan, draft, and revise your paragraph. For its sentences, create focused snapshot images of anything included in your description, pictures that enable your readers to see clearly every aspect and detail of what you are describing.

- Just as the authors' sentences in the previous samples use S-V splits, within your paragraph <u>use S-V splits and other sentence-composing tools</u>, <u>including openers</u>.

- For your S-V splits and openers, use at least one word, one phrase, one dependent clause as tools.

- Include at least ten sentences, varied in length but including some containing over twenty words.

- Exchange your rough draft with drafts of other students in your class to get suggestions for improvement. Use suggestions to revise your paragraph to make it better.

- Publish your writing by reading your paragraph to the class or posting it online or some other way so that you'll have lots of readers—maybe as a paragraph for your own novel!

Tip for Better Revising: Look for places to use openers and S-V splits to add substance, savvy, and style to your writing.

REVIEW

An S-V split is a word, phrase, or dependent clause separating a subject from its verb.

PREVIEW

You'll learn another good place to put words, phrases, or dependent clauses. It's called a closer because it ends the sentence.

THE CLOSER

Everybody likes a good ending: for example, a happy event at the end of a story, a sunset at the end of the day, a scrumptious desert at the end of a meal. Sometimes, authors use tools at the end of a sentence because that's the best place for a lasting impression. Take a look at sentences without tools at the end, and then compare them to sentences with tools at the end called closers because they come at the closing of the sentence:

1a. The head of the tyrannosaur pulled away.

1b. The head of the tyrannosaur pulled away, <u>abruptly</u>.

Michael Crichton, Jurassic Park

2a. A man climbed out.

2b. A man climbed out, <u>thickset</u>, <u>chunky</u>, <u>grinning</u>, <u>wearing a flat cap and a raincoat flapping over rubber boots</u>.

Susan Cooper, The Grey King

3a. To my right is Gretchen.

3b. To my right is Gretchen, <u>who has got her chin jutting out</u>, <u>as if it would win the race all by itself</u>.

Toni Cade Bambara, "Raymond's Run"

4a. That face belonged to Phoebe Winterbottom.

4b. That face belonged to Phoebe Winterbottom, <u>a girl with a powerful imagination</u>, <u>who would become my friend</u>, and <u>who would have many peculiar things happen to her</u>.

Sharon Creech, Walk Two Moons

5a. Hardly anyone goes to sleep.

5b. Hardly anyone goes to sleep, <u>because the start is very early in the</u> <u>morning,</u> <u>before it gets light,</u> <u>and because everyone has so much to</u> <u>prepare</u>.

Joseph Krumgold, . . . And Now Miguel

A closer is any tool at the end of the sentence. Closers can be *words*, *phrases*, or *clauses*. Below are examples from the above sentences.

WORDS

- *abruptly*
- *thickset*
- *chunky*
- *grinning*

PHRASES

- *wearing a flat cap and a raincoat flapping over rubber boots*
- *a girl with a powerful imagination*

CLAUSES

- *who has got her chin jutting out*
- *as if it would win the race all by itself*

- *who would become my friend*
- *who would have many peculiar things happen to her*
- *because the start is very early in the morning*
- *before the day gets light*
- *because everyone has so much to prepare*

ACTIVITY 1: MATCHING

Match the closer with its sentence. Write out each sentence, inserting the closer at the caret mark (^) and underlining it. Name the kind of closer—*word*, *phrase*, or *dependent clause*. **Punctuation:** Use a comma before each closer.

Sentence	Closer
1. My sister turned from the river and closed her eyes, ^ . Fanny Billingsley, *Chime*	a. as if it were an arrow or a spear
2. Alice laughed, and the sound was all silver, ^ . Stephenie Meyer, *New Moons*	b. as though she could wish away the river, and the barge on the river, and Eldric on the barge
3. She also had to watch our three chickens, ^ . Laurence Yep, *Dragonwings*	c. who loved to wander away from our farm
4. Lyra felt the force of his glance almost as if it had physical form, ^ . Philip Pullman, *The Golden Compass*	d. singing away, happy as a bull frog
5. He kept time with one hand, ^ . Joseph Krumgold, *Onion John*	e. a wind chime

ACTIVITY 2: COMBINING

Combine each pair of sentences by making the underlined part a closer for the other sentence. The result is the sentence the author wrote—one sentence instead of two to say the same thing! Don't forget the comma before the closer.

EXAMPLE

Two Sentences

Flung across her shoulder was her magician's bag. It was <u>marked with the symbol of the lion goddess</u>.

One Sentence with Closer

Flung across her shoulder was her magician's bag, <u>marked with the symbol of the lion goddess</u>.

Rick Riordan, *The Throne of Fire*

WORDS

1. I jumped to my feet. I was <u>thunderstruck</u>.
   Antoine de Saint-Exupéry, *The Little Prince*

2. Abruptly, with a metallic scraping shriek, the car fell from the tyrannosaur's jaws. This happened <u>sickeningly</u>.
   Michael Crichton, *Jurassic Park*

3. Blue Elk went out. He was <u>hurt and angry</u>.

    Hal Borland, *When the Legends Die*

4. On the fog comes. It was <u>silent and steady and flat</u>.

    Suzanne Collins, *Catching Fire*

5. A stillness hovered in the high air. The stillness was <u>soft</u>, <u>quiet</u>, <u>peaceful</u>.

    Mildred D. Taylor, *Roll of Thunder, Hear My Cry*

PHRASES

6. It was night now. The night was <u>bright with moon fragment and stars and northern glow</u>.

    Paul Gallico, *The Snow Goose*

7. My heart flutters. My heart is <u>a large bird trapped in my chest</u>.

    Lisa Luedeke, *Smashed*

8. A poem circles back on itself. A poem does this while <u>eating its own tail and making you guess what it means</u>.

    Fanny Billingsley, *Chime*

9. Their heads were covered with wigs of European hair. The wigs were <u>curled in the latest fashion,</u> <u>and bound with ropes of pearls,</u> <u>rubies, and diamonds</u>.

    Margaret Landon, *Anna and the King of Siam*

10. The beagle came barreling toward me. It came toward me with <u>legs going lickety-split,</u> <u>long ears flopping,</u> <u>tail sticking up like a flagpole</u>.

    Phyllis Reynolds Naylor, *Shiloh*

CLAUSES

11. The thunder and lightning were frightening. This happened <u>while the rain came in gusts and torrents</u>.

Kate Shelley, "Iowa Heroine"

12. Dicey was up and dressed, washed and fed, and out the door, with the day's work outlined in her head. Dicey did all of that <u>before anyone else stirred in the silent house</u>.

Cynthia Voigt, *Seventeen Against the Dealer*

13. Around her neck was a thick silver chain. It was a chain <u>on which hung a dark red pendant the size of a baby's fist</u>.

Cassandra Clare, *City of Bones*

14. This girl suffered through Brownies with me. She was the one <u>who taught me how to swim</u>, <u>who understood about my parents</u>, <u>who didn't make fun of my bedroom</u>.

Laurie Halse Anderson, *Speak*

15. Down the dark path rode Sir Gawain into the valley of despair. Sir Gawain did this <u>because it was his sworn duty to go this day to the Green Chapel and offer himself to the Green Knight</u>, <u>who awaited him there</u>.

Katherine Paterson, *Park's Quest*

ACTIVITY 3: UNSCRAMBLING

Unscramble both lists of sentence parts to imitate the same model. Write out each imitation sentence, underline its closer, and tell the types: *word*, *phrase*, or *clause*. **Note:** *Some sentences have more than one closer.*

EXAMPLE

Model to Imitate: They were sitting outside a curbside cafe on Dong Khai Street, watching the local teenagers circle the square on mopeds.

Eoin Colfer, *Artemis Fowl*

List One	List Two
a. was walking around the scene of the robbery	**a.** observing the many passengers lining the gates of platforms
b. assessing the likely signs indicating the method of entry	**b.** they
c. the detective	**c.** were waiting inside the train station in New York City
Imitation: The detective was walking around the scene of the robbery, <u>assessing the likely signs indicating the method of entry</u>. (*phrase closer*)	**Imitation:** They were waiting inside the train station in New York City, <u>observing the many passengers lining the gates of platforms</u>. (*phrase closer*)

First Model: An old abandoned water tower stood on the horizon, rusty and scary.

Stephen King, "The Body"

1a. and stained	**2a.** a new backpack
1b. a discarded leather glove	**2b.** sleek
1c. torn	**2c.** was on the display
1d. lay on the ground	**2d.** and stylish

Second Model: Then he let go and plunged, running, sliding, and falling down into the ravine.

Virginia Hamilton, *M. C. Higgins, the Great*

3a. entertaining, thrilling	**4a.** and posed
3b. suddenly she opened her mouth	**4b.** and looking straight into the camera
3c. and sweeping out over the audience	**4c.** preening, smiling
3d. and sang	**4d.** now the model sauntered out

Third Model: Lucy immediately stepped into the wardrobe among the coats, leaving the door open, because she knew that it is very foolish to shut oneself into any wardrobe.

C. S. Lewis, *The Chronicles of Narnia*

5a. holding his head up	**6a.** Shirley
5b. because he thought that it was very important to demonstrate his confidence before the game	**6b.** keeping her guard up
5c. Logan	**6c.** since she thought that it was certainly smart to protect herself in any crowd
5d. quickly walked onto the field among the team	**6d.** carefully waded into the crowd of her fans

Fourth Model: We walked toward the classrooms together, the three of us in a row, trusting that the tide of classmates would part enough to let us by.

John Green, *Paper Towns*

7a. hoping that the noise of others would quiet down to let them talk	**8a.** raced onto the field together
7b. the parents	**8b.** the twenty of them as a team
7c. the two of them in a huddle	**8c.** knowing that their score in the game must be big enough to secure the playoffs
7d. sat down in the audience together	**8d.** the Panthers

Fifth Model: Charles Wallace, in yellow footed pajamas, lay on the foot of Meg's big brass bed, his small nose looking puffy and red, his head pillowed on the shiny black bulk of the dog.

Madeleine L'Engle, *A Wind in the Door*

9a. Brooks Powell	**10a.** in bright red bathing suit
9b. his feet planted on the lush green grass of the yard	**10b.** his toddler face looking tan and happy
9c. his costumed biceps appearing small but firm	**10c.** sat on the edge of Cape May's spacious white beach
9d. stood in the yard of his parents' welcoming suburban house	**10d.** Nate Wilkinson
9e. in Halloween Superman regalia	**10e.** his feet burrowing into the loose light sand of the beach

ACTIVITY 4: IMITATING

Each model sentence has more than one closer. Match the imitation with its model sentence. Then write your own imitation of the entire model—*not just the closers*—about something from your imagination or from a TV show, movie, story, or book.

MODEL SENTENCES

1. My golden goat Cheetah at my side, I climbed toward home, urging the straggling sheep along with my stick.

   Laura Resau and Maria Virginia Farinango, *The Queen of Water*

2. She was sitting on the front steps of her new house, her elbows propped on her knees, wearing heart-shaped sunglasses with white plastic frames.

   Sarah Dessen, *Someone Like You*

3. The pony's tracks were plain enough, dragging through the dew on the grass, tired tracks with little lines between them where the hoofs had dragged.

   John Steinbeck, *The Red Pony*

4. A young girl stood on the other side, twisting her nightcap from side to side in trembling hand, her face white with fear.

   Garth Nix, *Sabriel*

5. His body began to jerk and twitch as he crumpled, folding in on himself, growing smaller and smaller until he vanished entirely.

   Cassandra Clare, *City of Bones*

IMITATIONS

A. Her body started to move and rise as she levitated, lifting up off of her chair, rising higher and higher until she disappeared completely.

B. Maria was lying on the white sand of her favorite beach, her thoughts dipping into the past, weaving memory tapestries with light lovely moments.

C. His heavy raincoat over Bryan's head, he raced toward the school, holding the pouring rain away from his face.

D. The children's voices were loud enough, echoing across the playground at the school, excited sounds with few words between shrieks after the laughter had stopped.

E. A howling dog waited beyond the fence, raising its howl from low to high with increasing urgency, his head high toward the sky.

ACTIVITY 5: EXCHANGING

If the closer is a *word*, exchange it for a new word. If the closer is a *phrase*, exchange it for a new phrase. If the closer is a *dependent clause*, exchange it for a new dependent clause. Write out the complete sentence.

EXAMPLE: WORD CLOSER

Original Sentence: It was a girl, twisting in the dirt, hands gripping soil, **whimpering**.

Maggie Stiefvater, *Forever*

Sample Exchanges

- It was a girl, twisting in the dirt, hands gripping soil, **yelling**.

- It was a girl, twisting in the dirt, hands gripping soil, **playing**.

- It was a girl, twisting in the dirt, hands gripping soil, **crying**.

----

1. Edward smiled, **triumphant**.

    Stephenie Meyer, *New Moon*

2. The man toppled to one side, crumpled against the railing, **dead**.

    Robert Ludlum, *The Prometheus Deception*

3. The cars traveled Reynolds Street, **slowly** and **evenly**.

    Annie Dillard, *An American Childhood*

4. He was twenty-six, dark-haired and pleasant, **strong**, **willing**, and **loyal**.

    John Steinbeck, *Cannery Row*

5. In the beginning, there were dragons, **proud**, **fierce**, and **independent**.

    Christopher Paolini, *Inheritance*

EXAMPLE: PHRASE CLOSER

Original Sentence: When excited, the digger wasps give off a pungent odor, **a warning that they are ready to attack**.

Alexander Petrunkevitch, "The Spider and the Wasp"

Sample Exchanges

- When excited, the digger wasps give off a pungent odor, **a smell slightly resembling raw fish**.

- When excited, the digger wasps give off a pungent odor, **a sign that the wasp is getting ready to sting**.

- When excited, the digger wasps give off a pungent odor, **a characteristic only found in this species of wasps**.

----

6. She festooned our living room in green and yellow streamers, **the colors of my new school**.

   John Green, *Looking for Alaska*

7. In the faint light, she looked half-transparent, **bleached of color, wrapped in white like an angel**.

   Cassandra Clare, *City of Bones*

8. The rain was still coming down, **pattering against the windows** and **blurring the lights of the cars in the street outside**.

   Neil Gaiman, *Coraline*

9. They would return at sunset, **loaded down with bonito fish, their faces happy, their shouts filling the dusk**.

   Armstrong Sperry, *Call It Courage*

10. Kit could see the little wooden doll, **its arms sticking stiffly into the air, bobbing helplessly in the water a few feet away**.

    Elizabeth George Speare, *The Witch of Blackbird Pond*

- For your closers, use at least one word, one phrase, one dependent clause.

- Use closers for most of your sentences—or all of them, as in the author's paragraph.

- Create vivid and clear snapshots of all the details of the storm's destructiveness.

- Exchange your rough draft with drafts of other students in your class to get suggestions for improvement. Use suggestions to revise your paragraph to make it better.

- Publish your writing by reading your paragraph to the class or posting it online or some other way so that you'll have lots of readers—maybe as a paragraph for your own novel!

Tip for Better Revising: Look for places to use openers, S-V splits, and closers to add substance, savvy, and style to your writing.

REVIEW

A closer is a word, phrase, or dependent clause that ends a sentence.

PREVIEW

You've learned the three places in a sentence where authors add detail and elaboration: the opener, the S-V split, and the closer. Next, you'll learn how authors mix them within a sentence, and how you can do the same.

THE MIX

In the previous sections, you learned, practiced, and applied sentence openers, S-V splits, and closers. In this section, you'll do activities using a mixture of those places within sentences in paragraphs.

A mix is using two or three of the tool places—opener, S-V split, closer—within the same sentence. Mixes can be *words*, *phrases*, or *clauses*.

Based upon the popular futuristic Lockdown series by Alexander Gordon Smith, both of the following paragraphs describe the same incident: the main character, a teenage boy, Alex Sawyer, who, although innocent of murder, is in a horrible prison called "Furnace," a dark prison for young offenders buried beneath the earth's surface, a place of gruesome giants and beasts who prey upon the young inmates. In this paragraph, Alex and other boys attempting escape are pursued by a deformed beast. Notice how much more descriptive power is in the paragraph with sentence-composing tools used in various places: opener, S-V split, closer.

VERSION WITHOUT TOOLS

I was dead. My lungs were on fire. I couldn't even see where I was going anymore. Then I'd have been able to hear my breaths. I forced myself to run faster. Everywhere around me other kids were panicking. I didn't look back to see what was behind us. I could picture it in my head. Then the beast shrieked, and I started running again. I was history. I leaped up the last few steps. I staggered. Somehow I made it. The creature howled. I risked looking back through the bars. There was a scream, but I was safe.
(99 WORDS)

VERSION WITH TOOLS IN VARIOUS PLACES *(UNDERLINED)*

If I stopped running, I was dead. My lungs were on fire, <u>my heart pumping acid</u>, <u>every muscle in my body threatening to cramp</u>. I couldn't even see where I was going anymore, <u>my vision fading as my body prepared to give in</u>. <u>If the siren hadn't been hammering at my eardrums</u>, then I'd have been able to hear my breaths, <u>ragged and desperate</u>, <u>unable to pull in enough air to keep me going</u>. I forced myself to run faster, <u>the metal staircase rattling beneath my clumsy steps</u>. Everywhere around me other kids, <u>all bolting the same way to safety</u>, were panicking. I didn't look back to see what was behind us. <u>Instantly</u>, I could picture it in my head, <u>its demonic muzzle, silver eyes, and teeth like razor wire</u>. Then the beast, <u>through its wet throat</u>, shrieked, and I started running again <u>before I even knew I was doing it</u>. <u>If I was caught outside the cells</u>, I was history. I leaped up the last few steps, <u>hurtling down the narrow landing</u>. I staggered, <u>lurching forward</u>, <u>falling</u>. Somehow I made it, <u>swinging through the door before it slammed shut</u>, <u>the mechanism locking tight</u>. The creature howled, <u>a banshee's wail that made my skin crawl</u>. I risked looking back through the bars, <u>seeing its huge bulk bounding past my cell</u>, <u>no skin to hide its grotesque muscles</u>. <u>As it found another victim</u>, there was a scream, but I was safe. **(242 WORDS, <u>most of which are tools!</u>)**

Alexander Gordon Smith, *Lockdown*

TOOL PLACES BY POSITION

OPENERS

- *if I stopped running*
- *if the siren hadn't been hammering at my eardrums*
- *instantly*

- *if I was caught outside the cells*
- *as it found another victim*

S-V SPLITS

- *all bolting the same way to safety*
- *through its wet throat*

CLOSERS

- *my heart pumping acid*
- *every muscle in my body threatening to cramp*
- *my vision fading as my body prepared to give in*
- *ragged and desperate, unable to pull in enough air to keep me going*
- *the metal staircase rattling beneath my clumsy steps*
- *its demonic muzzle, silver eyes, and teeth like razor wire*
- *before I even knew I was doing it*
- *hurtling down the narrow landing*
- *lurching forward*
- *falling*
- *swinging through the door an instant before it slammed shut*
- *the mechanism locking tight*
- *a banshee's wail that made my skin crawl*
- *seeing its huge bulk bounding past my cell*
- *no skin to hide its grotesque muscles*

TOOL PLACES BY TYPE

WORDS

- *instantly*
- *ragged*
- *desperate*
- *falling*

PHRASES

- *all bolting the same way to safety*
- *its demonic muzzle, silver eyes, and teeth like razor wire*
- *through its wet throat*
- *my heart pumping acid*
- *every muscle in my body threatening to cramp*
- *my vision fading as my body prepared to give in*
- *unable to pull in enough air to keep me going*
- *the metal staircase rattling beneath my clumsy steps*
- *hurtling down the narrow landing*
- *lurching forward*
- *swinging through the door an instant*
- *the mechanism locking tight*
- *a banshee's wail that made my skin crawl*
- *seeing its huge bulk bounding past my cell*
- *no skin to hide its grotesque muscles*

CLAUSES

- *if I stopped running*
- *if the siren hadn't been hammering at my eardrums*
- *if I was caught outside the cells*
- *as it found another victim*
- *before I even knew I was doing it*
- *before it slammed shut*

Clearly, the paragraph with tools is much stronger than the paragraph without tools. Authors often add tools in a mix of places within sentences to elaborate meaning and enhance the style of their sentences and paragraphs. Using a mix of places will also strengthen your writing.

ACTIVITY 1: MATCHING

These sentences mix tool places—openers, S-V splits, closers. Enrich each sentence by adding sentence tools at the mixed places (^). Write out and punctuate the sentence, underline the tools, identify each tool (*word, phrase, clause*) and name where it occurs (*opener, S-V split, closer*).

Sentences	Tools
1. ^ , Grant collapsed back, ^ . Michael Crichton, *Jurassic Park*	**a.** his muscles flexing tightly against his thin shirt and the sweat popping off his skin like oil on water / where he set it down as gently as a sleeping child
2 . ^ , the car jolted forward so fast that my body slammed into the black leather seat, ^ . Stephenie Meyer, *Breaking Dawn*	**b.** listening / unknown to the others

3. Perhaps each of them, ^ , glimpsed through that window a private world, ^ .
 	
    Elizabeth George Speare,
    The Witch of Blackbird Pond
	c. exhausted from rowing / his chest heaving

4. A man in furs, ^ , stood in the foreground, ^ . Philip Pullman, *The Golden Compass*	**d.** engine snarling like a hunting panther / my stomach flattening against my spine

5. ^ , he lifted the truck in one fluid, powerful motion until the front was several inches off the ground and slowly walked it to the left of the road, ^ .
 	
    Mildred D. Taylor,
    Roll of Thunder, Hear My Cry
	e. his face hardly visible in the deep hood of his garment / with his hand raised as if in greeting

In these next five, continue matching sentences and tools.

6. ^ , the neighbor's dog, ^ , came into the house uninvited and unannounced and lifted his leg on the dining-room table, ^ . Kate DiCamillo, *The Miraculous Journey*	**f.** slowly / spreading towards the man and midwife / who scuttled to the other side of the fire to get away
7 . ^ , I plunged my hand deeper into the darkness inside the wall containing bees, ^ , ^ . Laura Resau and Maria Virginia Farinango, *The Queen of Water*	**g.** as I opened the door / because the room was so filled with smoke that the light of the lamp upon the table was blurred by it
8. ^ , Ben had been my best friend since fifth grade, ^ . John Green, *Paper Towns*	**h.** in the half-light of dawn / searching for honey from bees / dreaming of golden treasures
9. ^ , a chill mist began to rise from his body ^ , ^ . Garth Nix, *Sabriel*	**i.** while Abilene was at school / a male brindled boxer inexplicably named Rosie, / spraying the white tablecloth with urine

10. My first impression, ^ , was that a fire had broken out, ^ . Sir Arthur Conan Doyle, *The Hound of the Baskervilles*	**j.** a small olive-skinned creature who had hit puberty but never hit it very hard / when we both finally owned up to the fact that neither of us was likely to attract anyone else as a best friend

ACTIVITY 2: ARRANGING

Following are stripped-down sentences, with the sentence-composing tools from the original sentences underneath. In the original sentences, the tools occupied *mixed places*. Insert the tools in *mixed places*. Punctuate and write out the sentence, and name the type of tools (*word, phrase, clause*) and places (*opener, S-V split, closer*). Finally, using your arranged sentence as a model, write an imitation.

EXAMPLE

Basic Sentence: The vampires waited.

Tools to Arrange

a. with eerie patience

b. outside

Sample Student Result: Outside, the vampires, with eerie patience, waited. (word opener, phrase S-V split)

Student Imitation: Nearby, the children, in clever costumes, paraded.

Original Sentence: Outside, the vampires waited, with eerie patience.

Claudia Gray, *Evernight*

Note: *As in the student sample above, the arrangement might differ from the original—and perhaps be better!*

----

1. My house came into view.

   a. past the corn and potato fields

   b. looking small and weak against the mountains towering behind it

   Laura Resau and Maria Virginia Farinango, *The Queen of Water*

2. Gwydion sat with his knees drawn up.

   a. his back against an enormous elm

   b. watchful

   Lloyd Alexander, *The Book of Three*

3. Nathaniel slipped the rope from the mooring and leaped nimbly to his place with the crew.

   a. coming back down the road on a run

   b. as they pulled away from the wharf

   Elizabeth George Speare, *The Witch of Blackbird Pond*

4. Our clan has splintered.

   a. the pieces being absorbed by rival factions

   b. the Plain Janes

   Laurie Halse Anderson, *Speak*

5. Margaret Murry sat on the foot of her bed and watched the trees.

   a. tossing in the frenzied lashing of the wind

   b. in her attic bedroom

   c. wrapped in an old patchwork quilt

   Madeleine L'Engle, *A Wrinkle in Time*

6. Tim was knocked flat on the seat.

   a. his mouth warm with blood

   b. after the tyrannosaur's head crashed against the hood of the Land Cruiser and shattered the windshield

   c. blinking in the darkness

   Michael Crichton, *Jurassic Park*

7. The sun came up over the lake, and he noted how beautiful it was.

   a. the new sun shining like gold

   b. the mist rising

   c. as he sipped his coffee

   Gary Paulsen, *Brian's Winter*

8. The doctor was a dapper and serious fifty-six-year-old surgeon.

   Rebecca Skloot, *The Immortal Life of Henrietta Lacks*

   a. brilliant

   b. who walked with an extreme limp from an ice-skating accident more than a decade earlier

   c. one of the top cervical cancer experts in the country

9. I saw the big gray dog.

    a. sucking the juice from the cactus

    b. in the brush above me

    c. while I was resting there

    d. the leader of the wild pack

    Scott O'Dell, *Island of Blue Dolphins*

10. The snake slithered straight toward Justin Finch-Fletchley and raised itself again.

    a. hissing furiously

    b. fangs exposed

    c. poised to strike

    d. enraged

    J. K. Rowling, *Harry Potter and the Chamber of Secrets*

REVIEW OF TOOLS

In this review of tool places within sentences you'll practice being a sentence-structure acrobat, with versatility and variety as your goals, through using tool places effectively: *openers*, *S-V splits*, *closers*—and *mixes*. You'll create tools to add to sentences by authors. For all your tools, pretend you are the author, composing a sentence that will actually appear in a book that might become a best-seller you helped to write!

ACTIVITY 1: EXPANDING

Each sentence that follows is a stripped-down version of an author's sentence. At the caret marks (^) add a variety of tool types (*word*, *phrase*, *clause*) and lengths (*short*, *medium*, *long*).

EXAMPLE

Basic Sentence: ^ , Harry spotted Fred and George Weasley, ^ .

Sample Student Result: <u>Overhearing the muffled conversation in the vestibule of the dining hall</u>, Harry spotted Fred and George Weasley, <u>whose faces were pale and eerie in the moonlight</u>.

Original: <u>Through the thicket of legs around him</u>, Harry spotted Fred and George Weasley, <u>wrestling the rogue Bludger into a box</u>.

J. K. Rowling, *Harry Potter and the Chamber of Secrets*

---

1. Royce paused a moment, ^ , ^ .

George R. R. Martin, *A Game of Thrones*

2. ^ and ^ , M. C. didn't mind being by himself.

Virginia Hamilton, *M. C. Higgins, the Great*

3. She was just standing in the doorway, ^ , ^ .

Sarah Dessen, *Lock and Key*

4. ^ , she got up in her nice hazy daze and wandered away from the dike, ^ .

Meindert DeJong, *The Wheel on the School*

5. ^ , she plunged headlong over the side of the boat, ^ .

Elizabeth George Speare, *The Witch of Blackbird Pond*

6. ^ , I pressed my face into my goat's fur, ^ , ^ .

Laura Resau and Maria Virginia Farinango, *The Queen of Water*

7. ^ , ^ , Michael sat on a blanket, ^ .

J. M. Coetzee, *Life and Times of Michael K*

8. ^ , ^ , ^ , Mafatu awoke and sat upright.

Armstrong Sperry, *Call It Courage*

9. ^ , she turned back to Simon, ^ , ^ , ^ .

Cassandra Clare, *City of Bones*

10. Then I saw her, ^ , ^ , ^ , ^ .

Suzanne Collins, *The Hunger Games*

ACTIVITY 2: EXPANDING THREE WAYS

To review tool types, places, and lengths, expand each sentence at the caret mark (^) **three different ways** as in the examples. For your tools, create content that links to the interesting content of the rest of the sentence.

EXAMPLES

Basic Sentence

Twenty-four letters to Harry found their way into the house.

Adding Sentence Parts as Openers

1. WORD: <u>Incredibly</u>, twenty-four letters to Harry found their way into the house.

2. PHRASE: <u>A record number for one day's delivery</u>, twenty-four letters to Harry found their way into the house.

3. CLAUSE: <u>Although they arrived against the wishes of Vernon and Petunia Dursley</u>, twenty-four letters to Harry found their way into the house.

Adding Sentence Parts as S-V Splits

4. WORD: Twenty-four letters to Harry, <u>encrypted</u>, found their way into the house.

5. PHRASE: Twenty-four letters to Harry, <u>addressed in code intelligible only to Harry</u>, found their way into the house.

6. CLAUSE: Twenty-four letters to Harry, <u>because he snuck them in from the mailbox</u>, found their way into the house.

Adding Sentence Parts as Closers

7. WORD: Twenty-four letters to Harry found their way into the house, <u>miraculously</u>.

8. PHRASE: Twenty-four letters to Harry found their way into the house, <u>covered with dirt from Uncle Vernon's attempt to bury them in the back yard</u>.

9. CLAUSE: Twenty-four letters to Harry found their way into the house, <u>which contained twenty-four rooms, twenty-four windows, and twenty-four doors but only one floor</u>.

Adding Sentence Parts at All Three Places

10. <u>At the final count</u>, twenty-four letters to Harry, <u>none with return addresses</u>, found their way into the house, <u>delivered secretly by Dudley in exchange for Harry's offer to transform Dudley into a handsome prince</u>.

11. <u>Amazingly</u>, twenty-four letters to Harry, <u>through the invisible courier hired from the wizard directory</u>, found their way into the house, <u>to the astonishment and furor of Uncle Vernon</u>.

12. <u>Materializing out of nothing through Harry's special use-once-only spell for undetectable mail delivery</u>, twenty-four letters to Harry, <u>all written in invisible typing readable only with Harry's spectacles</u>, found their way into the house, <u>the final letter warning Harry of the presence of Lord Valdemort in Harry's neighborhood</u>.

Original Sentence

Twenty-four letters to Harry found their way into the house, rolled up and hidden inside each of the two dozen eggs that their very confused milkman had handed Aunt Petunia through the living room window.

J. K. Rowling, *Harry Potter and the Sorcerer's Stone*

PART ONE: OPENERS

Like examples 1–3 above, expand this same sentence three different ways at the beginning of the sentence.

^ , Sadako felt a pang of fear.

Eleanor Coerr, *Sadako and the Thousand Paper Cranes*

PART TWO: S-V SPLITS

Like examples 4–6 above, expand this same sentence three different ways at the middle of the sentence.

Boysie, ^ , heard the door shut and came to the living room.

Betsy Byars, *The Summer of the Swans*

PART THREE: CLOSERS

Like examples 7–9 above, expand this same sentence three different ways at the end of the sentence.

He began edging backwards out of the cave, ^ .

Robert Lipsyte, *The Contender*

PART FOUR: ALL THREE PLACES (MIX)

Like examples 10–12 above, expand this same sentence three different ways at the beginning, the middle, and the end of the sentence. Use whatever tool types and lengths work best.

^ , Romey, ^ , aimed at the rattlesnake and blew its head off, ^ .

Bill and Vera Cleaver, *Where the Lilies Bloom*

BUILDING STRONGER PARAGRAPHS

Write a paragraph describing an unusual real or imaginary person—as in the following paragraph from the Newberry Prize–winning novel *Kira-Kira* by Cynthia Kadohata.

WRITING PROCESS

Researching: Study the model paragraph that follows and identify all underlined tools (*word, phrase, clause*) and their places (*opener, S-V split, closer*).

Model Paragraph

(1) Uncle Katsuhisa was an odd fish. (2) He was as loud as my father was quiet. (3) <u>When he wasn't even talking</u>, he made a lot of noise, <u>clearing his throat</u> and <u>sniffing</u> and <u>tapping his fingers</u>. (4) <u>Sometimes</u>, <u>for no apparent reason</u>, Uncle Katsuhisa, <u>a practical joker</u>, would suddenly stand up and clap his hands together really loudly. (5) <u>After he got everyone's attention</u>, he would just sit down again. (6) <u>When he was thinking</u>, he even made noise. (7) <u>When he was deep in thought</u>, he had a way of turning his ears inside out so they looked deformed. (8) <u>When his ears came undone</u>, they would make a popping sound. (9) A button-like scar marked one side of his nose. (10) <u>When he was a boy in Japan</u>, he, <u>supposedly</u>, was attacked by giant crows, <u>who tried to steal his nose</u>. The crows of Japan are famous for being mean. <u>Anyway</u>, that was the story Lynn told me.

Cynthia Kadohata, *Kira-Kira*

Prewriting: Think of a real or imaginary person with an obvious and interesting signature characteristic. Like the model paragraph, begin your paragraph with a short preview sentence that identifies that characteristic. Use this format: [NAME OF PERSON] was *clumsy, smart, sneaky, silly, awkward, deceitful, popular, unpopular, fearless, fearful, mean, crazy, weird, funny, shy, creepy*—or some other characteristic typical of the person.

Drafting: Draft a paragraph giving several examples of the person's unusual, interesting characteristic. In the model paragraph, the author provides numerous examples of the uncle being an "odd fish." Within your paragraph, use tools of different types and in different places. Here are examples from the model paragraph:

Words

- *sniffing* (closer)
- *sometimes* (opener)
- *supposedly* (S-V split)
- *anyway* (opener)

Phrases

- *clearing his throat* (closer)
- *tapping his fingers* (closer)
- *for no apparent reason* (opener)
- *a practical joker* (S-V split)

Clauses

- *when he wasn't even talking* (opener)
- *after he got everyone's attention* (opener)
- *when he was thinking* (opener)

- *when he was deep in thought* (opener)

- *when his ears came undone* (opener)

- *when he was a boy in Japan* (opener)

- *who tried to steal his nose* (closer)

Peer responding and revising: Exchange your draft with other students in your class for suggestions to improve your paragraph, and give them suggestions, too. Then revise several times until your paragraph is finished.

Creating a Title: Choose a title that your readers won't understand until after they read your paragraph. *Example for the model paragraph:* "An Odd Fish."

Having imagination, you take an hour to write
a paragraph that if you were unimaginative
would take one minute.

—Franklin Pierce Adams, *journalist*

Countries, states, cities, have boundaries. Home owners have them. Sentences have them, too. It's possible to have too much of a good thing—and too little. The goal is "just enough." When sentences are "out of bounds," they go too far, or don't go far enough. In other words, they don't stick to their boundaries. Just as when states, sports, houses don't honor their proper boundaries, problems occur. With sentences, there can be three kinds of boundary problems: run-ons, comma splices, and fragments.

TOO LITTLE SENTENCE: FRAGMENTS

A fragment is "too little" sentence: a sentence part mistakenly written like a complete sentence—capital letter at the beginning, period at the end.

Because readers expect a whole sentence when they see something that begins with a capital letter and ends with a period, fragments confuse readers: a fragment is just a *piece* of a sentence. Readers expect a *whole* sentence.

EXAMPLES OF FRAGMENTS

Each of the two lists contain fragments, and only one sentence. Which is that sentence? Why?

List One

1. Which he may have fed to the farm's omnivorous raccoon dogs.

2. The site of that horse's greatest performance.

3. At daybreak on a fine summer's morning, when the Riddle House had still been well kept and impressive.

4. Insisting that his muddy yellow coat matched the bright flower.

5. I sleep with two cats, who sleep on my legs.

ACTIVITY 1: CORRECTING FRAGMENTS

Each sentence part that follows is a fragment because it's not connected to a complete sentence. Connect each fragment to a complete sentence.

EXAMPLE

Fragment: because the weather was unbearably hot

Sentence part of complete sentence: Because the weather was unbearably hot, Tamara stopped jogging and walked the rest of the way back to the dorm.

Begin a complete sentence with these sentence parts:

1. because during the gigantic sale we bought in bulk to save money
2. to find out if I would enjoy it
3. around noon after we had arrived at the airport and rented a car
4. now abandoned by its owner because of the flood from the hurricane
5. constantly intentionally straying off the topic during our conversation

End a complete sentence with these sentence parts:

6. one of the funniest but most intelligent teachers I've ever had
7. and as a result Jasper aced the exam in psychology class
8. which was the sleekest car Mariah had ever driven
9. a price higher than the one advertised
10. arranging a much more manageable schedule to balance work and study

ACTIVITY 2: INSERTING FRAGMENTS INTO SENTENCES

The list on the right contains fragments to insert at the caret (^) in the appropriate sentence on the left, where they then become tools.

Sentences	Fragments
1. She was a big, good-looking girl, ^ . Annie Proulx, "The Indian Wars Refought"	**a.** almost as much as he was relieved to be done speaking
2. Mortenson appreciated the applause, ^ . Greg Mortenson, *Three Cups of Tea*	**b.** with her little lacquer brush, while the phone was ringing
3. ^ , he opened the door to the room and dropped off to sleep on the bed the old lady died in. Toni Morrison, *Beloved*	**c.** buxom and curvaceous, with dusty black hair, except for a fringe of bleached blond bangs, pulled into a pony-tail that slapped her between her shoulder blades when she ran
4. ^ , she went over the nail of her little finger to accentuate the line of the moon. J. D. Salinger, "A Perfect Day for Bananafish"	**d.** irritable and longing for rest
5. ^ , they never give their foster mother trouble, and she never loses her placid behaviour or her sense of authority of her litter. Yann Martel, *Life of Pi*	**e.** though the lion cubs grow to become larger than the dogs used as their foster mothers, and far more dangerous

ACTIVITY 3: DETECTING FRAGMENTS

One way to easily spot fragments is to read backward. Read from the end of what you've written back to the beginning. Sentence parts that are fragments will instantly get your attention. Read the following paragraph backward to spot fragments, and then, to eliminate them, join each fragment to the sentence where it belongs.

(1) The delivery truck pulled up in front of the house. (2) A townhouse at the end of the block across from the park. (3) Parking in front of the house with the engine running. (4) The delivery man exited the truck and walked up the sidewalk to the porch. (5) But noticed that the front door was wide open. (6) Reluctant to enter the home unannounced, he knocked on the door. (7) Hoping that someone would hear him and come to the porch to accept delivery of the package. (8) Something that neared the weight limit for packages set by his company. (9) There was no response. (10) Yelling into the house, he identified himself as a delivery man. (11) And asked if someone could please come to the front door to take delivery of the package. (12) When no one appeared, he decided to leave a notice of attempted delivery. (13) Rather than leave the package on the porch where it might be unsafe.

ACTIVITY 4: ELIMINATING FRAGMENTS

The next paragraph is difficult to read because of fragments. Revise the paragraph to eliminate all fragments. Don't add or delete words. Just connect each fragment to the sentence where it belongs—the sentence before or after the fragment, whichever makes more sense. At many of the connection points, a comma is needed.

(1) Most hurricanes don't cause massive destruction, passing through an area with little or no damage, injuries, or fatalities. (2) There are exceptions. (3) That, because of their devastating effects,

set records. (4) The worst hurricane worldwide on record occurred in 2005, Hurricane Katrina in the United States. (5) Which struck Louisiana and Mississippi, mainly their coastal areas on the Gulf of Mexico. (6) With loss of lives estimated at over 1900 victims, and property damage over $100 billion dollars. (7) Although Hurricane Katrina is the most devastating on record. (8) Katrina's winds were not the most intense in miles per hour. (9) That record is held by Hurricane Camille. (10) A storm that in 1969 raged in the North Atlantic at 190 miles per hour, with gusts as high as 210 miles per hour. (11) The strongest ever of any hurricane making landfall. (12) After skirting the coast of Cuba, it picked up speed in the Gulf of Mexico. (13) Then headed for the coast of Mississippi, and then to the mountains of Virginia. (14) One of only four hurricanes worldwide to reach winds of 190 miles per hour, and the only one of the four to cause widespread death and damage on landfall. (15) Estimates of the devastation include over 250 fatalities, with property damage costing billions of dollars.

TOO MUCH SENTENCE: COMMA SPLICES AND RUN-ONS

A *comma splice* is too much sentence, usually two sentences written incorrectly as one sentence, with just a comma splicing them together.

A *run-on* is also too much sentence. It is two sentences incorrectly written as one sentence, but with nothing between the two sentences to tell your readers where one sentence ends and the next sentence begins.

Your readers expect a clear boundary between two sentences telling where one sentence ends and the next sentence begins. Comma splices and run-ons lack that boundary. Both problems have "too much sentence," confusing your readers, who need sentence boundaries to tell where one sentence ends and the next sentence begins.

Comma splices and run-ons cause reading problems. If you get confused reading the following example, it's not your fault. It's the fault of the comma splice contained in the example. In the following paragraph, which is based upon *The Contender* by Robert Lipsyte, notice the place between the two bolded words. The comma splice happens there.

EXAMPLE OF A COMMA SPLICE

His heart pounding, his lungs inhaling and exhaling like a bellows, Alfred, lunging toward his opponent Jacobs in the third round with his left, swung but **missed, recovering** from the miss, he turned swiftly, aimed again, and this time connected squarely with Jacobs' jaw. (*Two sentences with just a comma between them*)

Likewise, you'll get confused reading the following example—a run-on. The confusion occurs at the same place—between *missed* and *recovering*.

EXAMPLE OF A RUN-ON

His heart pounding, his lungs inhaling and exhaling like a bellows, Alfred, lunging toward his opponent Jacobs in the third round with his left, swung but missed recovering from the miss, he turned swiftly, aimed again, and this time connected squarely with Jacobs' jaw. (*Two sentences with nothing between them*)

Note: *Sentence length has nothing to do with whether something is a run-on. If two sentences have no punctuation or words between them, it's a run-on, regardless of the length of the sentence. As you will see, something very short can be a run-on sentence, and something very long can be a correct sentence—not a run-on.*

A RUN-ON: The rain stopped the game continued. (*It's a run-on between "stopped" and "the game"—where the first sentence should end, and the second one begin.*)

NOT A RUN-ON: Slowly, his muscles flexing tightly against his thin shirt and the sweat popping off his skin like oil on water, he lifted the truck in one fluid, powerful motion until the front was several inches off the ground and slowly walked it to the left of the road, where he set it down as gently as a sleeping child. (*Even though very long, it is not a run-on sentence. It is one sentence.*)

Mildred D. Taylor, *Roll of Thunder, Hear My Cry*

> **Remember this:** A run-on sentence results from unclear sentence boundaries, not sentence length. In this worktext you'll see many very long sentences by authors. None of them is a run-on.

ELIMINATING COMMA SPLICES OR RUN-ONS

There are three ways to get rid of either a comma splice or a run-on.

1. MAKE TWO SENTENCES: *Use a period to end the first sentence, and a capital letter to start the next sentence.*

   His heart pounding, his lungs inhaling and exhaling like a bellows, Alfred, lunging toward his opponent Jacobs in the third round with his left, swung but missed. **Recovering** from the miss, he turned swiftly, aimed again, and this time connected squarely with Jacobs' jaw.

2. ADD A COMMA PLUS *and, but, or, so, for, or yet* TO JOIN THE SENTENCES.

   His heart pounding, his lungs inhaling and exhaling like a bellows, Alfred, lunging toward his opponent Jacobs in the third round with his left, swung but missed, **but** recovering from the miss, he turned swiftly, aimed again, and this time connected squarely with Jacobs' jaw.

3. USE A SEMICOLON BETWEEN THE SENTENCES: *A semicolon can replace a period if the two sentences are closely linked in meaning.*

His heart pounding, his lungs inhaling and exhaling like a bellows, Alfred, lunging toward his opponent Jacobs in the third round with his left, swung but missed; **recovering** from the miss, he turned swiftly, aimed again, and this time connected squarely with Jacobs' jaw.

ACTIVITY 5: ELIMINATING COMMA SPLICES AND RUN-ONS

Numbers 1–5 each contain a comma splice or a run-on. Revise each three times, each time using a different way from the three methods for eliminating comma splices and run-ons. For example, do number one three different ways, then number two three different ways, and so forth for all five.

1. In large metropolitan areas, GPS systems are a useful means of locating businesses, services, and products, the average customer would be lost without this aid.

2. Very overweight and stocky, Mr. Jackson didn't understand fully how his weight problem affected his health, his doctor, after giving him a physical, put him on a strict diet of fruits, vegetables, and lean meat.

3. I am almost ashamed to admit it I do enjoy reading a good book, one that is entertaining, one that stimulates my thinking, and one that captures my imagination.

4. The Internet, a powerful research tool, is technically very complex finding information almost at the speed of light is within the capability of anyone with a computer and Internet connection.

5. According to most literary scholars, the plays of Shakespeare were, in fact, written by William Shakespeare according to some brilliant people, including Sigmund Freud and Charles Dickens, they were possibly written by someone else who used Shakespeare's name.

ACTIVITY 6: AVOIDING COMMA SPLICES AND RUN-ONS

Add punctuation where needed to avoid a comma splice or run-on.

1a. When Mark Twain

1b. the famous author

1c. whose real name was Samuel Clemens

1d. was a boy of fourteen

1e. he thought his father was stupid

1f. when Twain reached twenty-one

1g. he was amazed how much his father had learned.

2a. Extremely arrogant and conceited

2b. Eric didn't comprehend how his overpowering style affected his lack of friends

2c. his mother

2d. after describing how to pay more attention to others

2e. told him to be considerate and stop bragging to everyone about his superiority

3a. Oatmeal

3b. that common breakfast cereal

3c. is not just for breakfast anymore

3d. mushy and semi-disgusting

3e. it's good for other things

3f. like putting in your little brother's shoes

3g. his baseball glove

3h. or his ears.

4a. As the storm

4b. a blizzard that had lasted two days

4c. covered the landscape

4d. blanketing everything in white

4e. Jake Slatterly

4f. whose job was to make sure provisions were ample

4g. began to worry

4h. he made a plan

4i. one that was by no means certain of success

4j. to hitch one of the horses to a wagon

4k. drive the little-used road on the other side of the mountain

4l. and

4m. with luck and a lot of prayers

4n. get to Dodge City to buy some grub and some whiskey

5a. Once in a while

5b. when summer is sunny and not too hot

5c. when the breezes refresh rather than disturb with too strong force

5d. after a swim in the pool or the lake

5e. it is refreshing to just air-dry in the warm breeze

5f. feel the caress of it against bare skin

5g. and close your eyes

5h. enjoying the beauty of nature's summer best

5i. on the contrary

5j. sharply contrasting

5k. are fierce winter winds

5l. chilling the bones

5m. and penetrating even layers and layers of clothes

5n. causing you to exit the outdoors

5o. and seek the warmth of inside

5p. thankful for protection from the harsh cold

ACTIVITY 7: IDENTIFYING BOUNDARY PROBLEMS

Read each item and then use the letter from this list to describe it:

    a. comma splice problem

    b. run-on problem

    c. both problems

    d. no problem

Next, revise any item that contains a comma splice, a run-on, or both problems.

    1. After Sandy left science class yesterday, her curiosity about global warming was high it was almost twice as high as before that interesting class.

2. When visiting the Internet, that electronic encyclopedia, Sandy was researching the debate on global warming, a fascinating topic, she found a lot of different opinions on it.

3. Part of the controversy concerns the causes of increased average temperatures globally, and whether these increases, which are minimal, are the result of improved measurement devices to record those increases.

4. Another controversy, perhaps the most prevalent, is whether temperature increases are part of normal variations that possibility is supported by many who have studied the issue, scientists are divided on this issue, leaning, however, mainly toward the belief that the cause is emission of greenhouse gases.

5. Throughout the world, scientists agree that there has been an increase in global surface temperatures, one induced by human activity, specifically the increased emissions.

6. In 1997, a document entitled the Kyoto Protocol affirmed that global warming poses a threat, reducing greenhouse gases among the world's industrial nations was its recommendation.

7. The Kyoto Protocol, a document signed by approximately 1500 of the world's top climatology scientists, including winners of the Nobel Prize in science, was a petition urging governments to enact binding laws, such legislation was designed to regulate industries that emit greenhouse gases during their manufacturing processes.

8. Adding to the controversy, skeptics believe that the issue is blown out of proportion, because they cite only minor fluctuations in global temperatures, no more than a few degrees variation over the last 10,000 years, these dissenters question the motives of serious supporters of the theory, those who call global warming a major threat to humanity.

9. Adding to the complexity of the issue are claims, usually made by industrial scientists, that manufacturers pressure scientists in their employ to downplay any findings that could be interpreted as supporting global warming, namely the belief that increased global temperatures, appearing only after the Industrial Revolution, are the result of unregulated emissions of greenhouse gases during manufacturing.

10. The controversy has produced some odd developments, one is that some scientists have made wagers about future average global temperatures, including two scientists who bet that in a future five-year period the average global temperature would not be higher than a past five-year period on the contrary, it would, they claim, be actually lower, thus refuting the claim of global warming.

ACTIVITY 8: CORRECTING BOUNDARY PROBLEMS

Comma splices and run-on problems happen when a writer fails to show a clear boundary between two sentences. Match the sentences from the right column to the sentences in the left column by making two sentences, or using a semicolon, or adding a comma plus *and* or *but*. Use each way at least once.

First Sentences	Next Sentences
1. Grown-ups never understand anything by themselves. Antoine de Saint-Exupéry, *The Little Prince*	a. they saved both his legs.
2. Harry had never believed he would meet a boy he hated more than Dudley. J. K. Rowling, *Harry Potter and the Sorcerer's Stone*	b. it was only a short one, a fretful childish whine muffled by passing through walls.

3. Bart was terribly mangled in the auto accident. Hal Borland, *When the Legends Die*	**c.** only in the full sunlight could you be seen, and then only by your shadow, and that would be shaky and faint.
4. It was another cry, but not quite like the one she had heard last night. Frances Hodgson Burnett, *The Secret Garden*	**d.** it is tiresome for children to be always and forever explaining things to them.
5. Gollum wanted the ring because it was a ring of power, and if you slipped that ring on your finger, you were invisible. J. R. R. Tolkien, *The Hobbit*	**e.** that was before he met Draco Malfoy.

BUILDING STRONGER PARAGRAPHS

Assignment: Revise the following paragraph to eliminate comma splices, run-ons, and fragments. Read your revised paragraph to make sure you corrected all of the sentence boundary problems.

WRITING PROCESS

Prewriting: The paragraph that follows contains all three problems: fragments, comma splices, run-ons. Study the paragraph to locate all boundary problems and identify their kind.

Drafting: Draft a rewrite of the paragraph that eliminates all sentence boundary problems.

(1) A locust resembles a grasshopper in appearance, but with shorter antennae. (2) Furthermore, grasshoppers are usually one inch long. (3) Whereas locusts are twice as long. (4) There are other

differences between the two species, mainly in behavior. Grasshoppers are solitary. (5) Loners content with little need for other grasshoppers. (6) Locusts, when they overpopulate and therefore lack enough food. (7) However, congregate in huge numbers, sometimes in the millions. (8) And evolve into a swarm in the sky resembling a black cloud. (9) In search of food, traveling on wind currents and descending on cotton, fruit, crops, and other vegetation. (10) Causing billions of dollars in lost income, locust swarms have a huge impact on an area's economy farmers and others, such as tree growers and landscapers, are especially hard-hit ever since recorded history, outbreaks of locusts have plagued humans. (11) Sometimes so many locusts amass in the sky, traveling in black bands miles wide, that they block out the sun. (12) They can travel hundreds of miles in a single day. (13) Because humans are almost helpless to prevent their attack. (14) Fortunately locust swarms are rare.

Peer responding and revising: Exchange your draft with other students in your class to achieve consensus on where the sentence boundary problems were. If your peer pointed out boundary problems you missed, revise to eliminate all boundary problems.

Creating a title: Create a clever title for your corrected paragraph about locusts.

BEST PARAGRAPHS

By studying how authors build their sentences, you practiced ways to improve your own sentences. You learned that "best sentences" are those with three parts: *a topic, a comment about that topic,* and *especially sentence-composing tools.*

What are "best paragraphs"? Paragraphs have three similar parts: *a topic, lots of comments about that same topic spread across many sentences,* and *especially sentence-composing tools like those used by authors.*

In the paragraph that follows, the topic is a young married couple named Amanda and John who get a stray cat from an animal shelter. The comments about the couple and the cat are spread across the seven-sentence paragraph. To illustrate the importance of sentence-composing tools within a paragraph, two versions of the paragraph are provided. In the first version, all of the sentence-composing tools are removed. In the second version, the author's tools are restored. Their restoration provides paragraph power.

PARAGRAPH WITHOUT SENTENCE-COMPOSING TOOLS

Amanda had fallen in love with a cat. The creature in question was an ancient twenty-three-pound one-eared Maine coon. The cat might have been bearable. He also insisted on sleeping in the couple's bed between their heads. Amanda didn't understand why John got so upset about a bit of dander on his pillow, and John didn't know how to explain that he had fully expected Amanda would adopt something. John when it died was as shattered as Amanda. They wept over the empty cat crate in the car. Amanda drew the blinds, crawled into bed, and stayed there for three days.

In the next version, the author uses lots of tools—*words, phrases, dependent clauses*—in the three places you learned earlier: the opener, the S-V split, and the closer.

In this restored paragraph, focus on the power of the sentence-composing tools and their locations within the sentences. Each sentence in the paragraph contains tools that add detail, meaning, variety, style, and texture to writing—hallmarks of good writing.

PARAGRAPH WITH SENTENCE-COMPOSING TOOLS

Amanda, <u>at the animal shelter</u>, had fallen in love with a cat. <u>Although they named the cat Magnificat</u>, the creature in question was an ancient twenty-three-pound one-eared Maine coon, <u>its tail permanently crooked</u>. <u>With also a flaking skin rash leaving him scaly and bald in places</u>, the cat might have been bearable. <u>However</u>, he also, <u>nightly</u>, insisted on sleeping in the couple's bed between their heads, <u>spreading his considerable heft between their pillows and batting at their heads if they didn't pet him enough</u>. Amanda didn't understand why John got so upset about a bit of dander on his pillow, and John didn't know how to explain that he had fully expected Amanda would adopt something, <u>a sweet little baby something</u>, <u>not a monstrous beast with a weepy eye</u>, <u>whose tongue stuck out perpetually because he had no teeth left to hold it in place</u>. <u>Yet</u>, <u>eight months later</u>, <u>when Magnificat's kidneys failed and they had to have him put down</u>, John, <u>when it died</u>, was as shattered as Amanda. They wept over the empty cat crate in the car, <u>clutching each other for a full twenty minutes before John felt composed enough to drive</u>. <u>Back home</u>, Amanda, <u>distraught</u> and <u>inconsolable</u>, drew the blinds, crawled into bed, and stayed there for three days.

Sara Gruen, *Ape House* (adapted)

Look at the paragraph's sentences side by side to see how tools make over the paragraph. For each tool, its type (word, phrase, clause) and place (opener, S-V split, closer) are indicated.

1a. Amanda had fallen in love with a cat.

1b. Amanda, <u>at the animal shelter</u>, had fallen in love with a cat. (***phrase S-V split***)

2a. The creature in question was an ancient twenty-three-pound one-eared Maine coon.

2b. <u>Although they named the cat Magnificat</u>, the creature in question was an ancient twenty-three-pound one-eared Maine coon, <u>its tail permanently crooked</u>. (***clause opener / phrase closer***)

3a. The cat might have been bearable.

3b. <u>With also a flaking skin rash leaving him scaly and bald in places</u>, the cat might have been bearable. (***phrase opener***)

4a. He also insisted on sleeping in the couple's bed between their heads.

4b. <u>However</u>, he also, <u>nightly</u>, insisted on sleeping in the couple's bed between their heads, <u>spreading his considerable heft between their pillows</u> and <u>batting at their heads</u> <u>if they didn't pet him enough</u>. (***word opener / word S-V split / phrase closer / phrase closer / clause closer***)

5a. Amanda didn't understand why John got so upset about a bit of dander on his pillow, and John didn't know how to explain that he had fully expected Amanda would adopt something.

5b. Amanda didn't understand why John got so upset about a bit of dander on his pillow, and John didn't know how to explain that he had fully expected Amanda would adopt something, <u>a sweet little baby something</u>, <u>not a monstrous beast with a weepy eye</u>, <u>whose tongue stuck out perpetually</u> <u>because he had no teeth left to hold it in place</u>. (***phrase closer / phrase closer / clause closer / clause closer***)

6a. John when it died was as shattered as Amanda.

6b. <u>Yet</u>, <u>eight months later</u>, <u>when Magnificat's kidneys failed and they had to have him put down</u>, John when it died was as shattered as Amanda. (***word opener / phrase opener / clause opener***)

7a. They wept over the empty cat crate in the car.

7b. They wept over the empty cat crate in the car, <u>clutching each other for a full twenty minutes</u> <u>before John felt composed enough to drive</u>. (***phrase closer / clause closer***)

8a. Amanda drew the blinds, crawled into bed, and stayed there for three days.

8b. <u>Back home</u>, Amanda, <u>distraught</u> and <u>inconsolable</u>, drew the blinds, crawled into bed, and stayed there for three days. (***phrase opener / word S-V split / word S-V split***)

THE NUMBERS

Sentences: Both paragraphs—the one without tools, and the one with tools—contain eight sentences.

Words: The paragraph without tools contains 102 words. The paragraph with tools contains 213 words, almost 50 percent more than the paragraph without tools.

Tools: Twenty tools are in the paragraph, including all types (*words*, *phrases*, *clauses*) and places (*openers*, *S-V splits*, and *closers*).

Conclusion: Almost one-half of the content of the original paragraph comes from the author's use of sentence-composing tools.

Paragraph Three: A young woman named Franny leaves her friend sitting at a table in a restaurant to find someplace where she can be alone to cry. She goes to the restaurant's restroom, where this paragraph takes place.

(1) [*short*], she went into the farthest and most anonymous-looking of the seven or eight enclosures, closed the door behind her, and, [short], manipulated the bolt to a locked position. (2) [*medium*], she sat down. (3) Then she placed her hands, [short], over her eyes and pressed the heels hard, [*long*]. (4) Her extended fingers, [*medium*], looked oddly graceful and pretty. (5) She cried for fully five minutes. (6) She cried without trying to suppress any of the noisier manifestations of grief and confusion, [*long*].

J. D. Salinger, *Franny and Zooey*

ACTIVITY 2: ADDING MULTIPLE SENTENCE PARTS

Some of the sentences in these paragraphs contained multiple sentence parts—more than one tool in a sentence. Others contained just one tool, and the rest none. For sentences with tools removed, create your own tools, using the word amount the author used: *short* (1–5), *medium* (6–10), *long* (10+). **Important:** Tools are sentence parts, not sentences, and need a comma to separate them from the rest of the sentence. Add sentence *parts*, not sentences.

EXAMPLE

Without Elaboration: [*short*], [*medium*], Sam went down after sunrise to the crashing waves.

With Elaboration (*samples*)

1. **Then, before anyone else had returned to the house**, Sam went down after sunrise to the crashing waves.

2. **Habitually, even though he had not eaten breakfast**, Sam went down after sunrise to the crashing waves.

3. **In darkness, when he had had a hard night sleeping**, Sam went down after sunrise to the crashing waves.

Original: **For weeks, while his brother and father slept**, Sam went down after sunrise to the crashing waves.

Holly Goldberg Sloan, *I'll Be There*

Paragraph One: A high school girl, alone in her house at the end of a quiet, dead end road, wakes at 2 a.m. to the sound of a car pulling into her driveway. Frightened, she gets out of bed and wonders what she should do.

(1) The car moved forward around the curve of the driveway as I tiptoed down the stairs, [long]. (2) I wondered if I should turn on the lights to let it be known I was there, [short], [short], [short]. (3) No, I thought. (4) See the car at first, at least. (5) [short], I waited.

Smashed by Lisa Luedeke

Paragraph Two: In this paragraph, a description of the dinosaur Tyrannosaurus rex, the author describes the complete animal, then focuses on specific parts of its anatomy, starting low, then gradually working upward to its head and then the details of the dinosaur's face. Tip: You might want to get an online image of a dinosaur for details of its appearance.

(1) It towered thirty feet above the trees, [*short*], [*long*]. (2) Each lower leg was a piston, [*medium*], [*medium*], [*long*]. (3) From the great breathing cage of the upper body, those two delicate arms dangled out front, [*long*], [*short*]. (4) The head itself, [*short*], lifted easily upon the sky.

(5) Its mouth gaped, [*medium*]. (6) Its eyes rolled, [*short*], [*medium*].

Ray Bradbury, "A Sound of Thunder" (adapted)

Paragraph Three: This describes a dashing, bold, and somewhat arrogant young knight before he is killed at age eighteen and turned into a "wight," an undead menacing creature with steely blue eyes and an ice-cold touch.

(1) Waymor Royce was the youngest son of an ancient house with too many heirs. (2) He was a handsome youth of eighteen, [*short*] and [*short*] and [*short*]. (3) [medium], the knight towered above Will and Gared on their smaller horses. (4) He wore black leather boots, black woolen pants, black moleskin gloves, and a fine supple coat of gleaming black ringmail over layers of black wool and boiled leather. (5) Waymor had been a Sworn Brother of the Night's Watch for less than half a year, but no one could say he had not prepared for his vocation, [*medium*]. (6) His sable cloak was his crowning glory, [*short*] and [*short*] and [*short*].

George R. R. Martin, *A Game of Thrones*

ACTIVITY 3: ADDING SIMILAR SENTENCE PARTS

Sometimes authors express several related ideas or bits of information in a similar way. This is called "parallel structure" because each part is similar (parallel) in importance, and so each part is built the same way (structure). In the following paragraphs, authors use the same word to begin each of the tools to create parallel structure. Using the word provided, create the rest of the tool, using the word amount the author used: *short* (1–5), *medium* (6–10), *long* (10+).

Before: My father told me to [*medium*], to [*long*], and to [*medium*].

After (*samples*)

1. My father told me **to get my grades up much higher in science, to go quickly to the nearest barber and get my hair cut to above my ears, and to be more responsible taking the garbage out.**

2. My father told me **to write down the grocery list, to take my little brother with me to the grocery store and not leave him there, and to put him in a car-cart there for security.**

3. My father told me **to be more careful with the laundry, to make sure that I put dark colors together and not mix them with light ones, and to use just warm not hot water to save money.**

Original: My father told me **to clean the irons with turpentine, to wash off the paint and the dirt and stuff that had got stuck to them, and to wrap them up in a rag for next year.**

Joseph Krumgold, . . . *And Now Miguel*

Paragraph One: Katie, the main character, often finds herself home alone, even at night. Her father disappeared when she was twelve, her mother works nights, then stays with a friend an hour away, and her little brother has taken permanent refuge at his best friend's house. In this paragraph, the author describes Katie's complex feelings of fear, anger, and loneliness.

Sunday night was long and dark and lonely. Every time I started to doze, a floorboard creaked or a tree branch scratched the roof, jolting me awake. I **hated** [*short*], **hated** [*medium*]. Sometimes, lying there at night, I felt like I'd explode if I couldn't go somewhere else, just be anywhere else other than this place—the place where my family had left me, one by one, to fend for myself.

Lisa Luedeke, Smashed

Paragraph Two: *Often threatened and insulted as she walks by girls and boys who bully her, a middle school girl is afraid on her way home from school.*

During the bitterly cold days of winter, the thirteen-year-old had gotten into the habit of counting the blocks until she was safe at home—**safe from** [*short*], **safe from** [*long*], **safe from** [*long*]. They all seemed to have something mean to say about her.

Traci L. Jones, Standing Against the Wind

Paragraph Three: *In this novel, set in the future in a horrible society, the main character Katniss Everdeen does all she can to protect her little sister Prim, even volunteering to take Prim's place when Prim is randomly selected to fight to the death in brutal games.*

I could never let that happen to Prim, sweet, tiny Prim, **who** [*medium*], **who** [*long*], **who** [*long*]. The community home would crush her like a bug, so I kept our predicament a secret.

Suzanne Collins, The Hunger Games

ACTIVITY 4: ADDING SENTENCES

Paragraphs in this activity have some of their sentences removed. Read each paragraph slowly several times, and then partner with the author to add your own sentences into the author's paragraph, sentences containing varied sentence-composing tools. Make sure what you write blends well with the rest of the author's paragraph in meaning, vocabulary, and style.

EXAMPLE

Reduced Paragraph

The enormous black iron bird cage was backed up against the corner garden wall and sheltered under a pergola with a tattered roof. **[ADD YOUR SENTENCE OF AT LEAST THIRTY WORDS.]** Judging from the noise, anyone nearby would have thought there were at least a dozen birds, but there were only five: a mynah with a saffron mask surrounding blood-red eyes; a white, sulfur-crested cockatoo; a noisy black grackle; a fearless yellow kiskadee; and a terrified foam-green honeycreeper who pulled at his own feathers.

Expanded Paragraph (*sample*)

The enormous black iron bird cage was backed up against the corner garden wall and sheltered under a pergola with a tattered roof. **Housed in the entry room of the castle, with an arched ceiling reaching fifty feet, high as a gothic cathedral, the cage was a bizarre accessory in the gloom of the castle's interior, a foreshadowing of the eccentricity of the master of the castle.** Judging from the noise, anyone nearby would have thought there were at least a dozen birds, but there were only five: a mynah with a saffron mask surrounding blood-red eyes; a white, sulfur-crested cockatoo; a noisy black grackle; a fearless yellow kiskadee; and a terrified foam-green honeycreeper who pulled at his own feathers.

Original Paragraph

The enormous black iron bird cage was backed up against the corner garden wall and sheltered under a pergola with a tattered roof. **At the sight or sound of a human being, the birds inside would flutter and scream as if they were on fire, grasping at the bars with their sharp claws.** Judging from the noise, anyone nearby would have thought there were at least a dozen birds, but there were only five: a mynah with a saffron mask surrounding blood-red eyes; a white, sulfur-crested cockatoo; a noisy black grackle; a fearless yellow kiskadee; and a terrified foam-green honeycreeper who pulled at his own feathers.

Kathleen O'Dell, *The Aviary*

PARAGRAPH ONE

At some point, bats would flit from the darkness out over the water to feed on the insects. George would stop fishing, because the bats struck at his fishing fly, and he had terrible notions of a frantic squeaking bat impaled on the barbed hook, trying to free itself and only breaking its own fragile wings in the process. Grabbing the bat and yanking the hook out would be unthinkable, so the only choice seemed as if it would be to run away, leaving the struggling animal on the end of the line, and to return the next morning to collect the rod and hope that a fox had happened along and eaten the bat—and not swallowed the hook along with the bat, so that it, too, now struggled somewhere in the woods, dragging the fishing pole by the taut line that now ran from its gut up through its throat and tore at the side of its mouth. **[ADD YOUR SENTENCE OF AT LEAST TWENTY WORDS.]**

Paul Harding, *Tinkers*

PARAGRAPH TWO

They were not long in the mountains before Larch accepted, bitterly, that it was an impossible hiding place. It wasn't the cold that was the problem, though autumn here was as raw as midwinter had been on the lord's estate. It wasn't the terrain either, though the scrub was hard and sharp, and they slept on rock every night, and there was no place even to imagine growing vegetables or grain. It was the predators. Not a week went by that Larch didn't have to defend against some attack: mountain lions, bears, wolves, the enormous birds, the raptors, with a wingspan twice the height of a man. **[ADD YOUR SENTENCE OF AT LEAST TWENTY WORDS.]** Larch's horse was lost one day to a pair of mountain lions.

Kristin Cashore, *Fire*

PARAGRAPH THREE

Hugo could hardly fall asleep. When he did, he dreamed about a terrible accident that occurred in the train station thirty-six years ago, which people still talked about. **[ADD YOUR SENTENCE OF AT LEAST TEN WORDS.]** A train had come into the station too fast. The brakes had failed, and the train slammed through the guardrail, jumped off the tracks, barreled across the floor of the station, rammed through two walls, and flew out the window, shattering the glass into a billion pieces. In his dream, Hugo was walking by himself outside the train station when he heard a loud crash and looked up, a train falling on him from the sky. **[ADD ANOTHER SENTENCE OF AT LEAST FIVE WORDS.]** *Afraid to go back to sleep*, Hugo climbed out of bed and got dressed.

Brian Selznick, The Invention of Hugo Cabret

PARAGRAPH FOUR

In my dream we were out over our heads in water. Chris's head went under, his mouth filling with water. **[ADD YOUR SENTENCE OF AT LEAST FIVE WORDS.]** Then he was dragged under again. Looking into the clear water, I could see two bloated corpses holding his ankles, their open eyes as blank and pupilless as the eyes of Greek statues. **[ADD ANOTHER SENTENCE OF AT LEAST FIVE WORDS.]** He held one hand up limply to me and voiced a screaming, womanish cry. Chris's scream turned into a bubbling water-choked gurgle as the corpses pulled him under again. Suddenly I felt a soft, rotted hand wrap itself around my calf and begin to pull. **[ADD ANOTHER SENTENCE OF AT LEAST TWENTY WORDS.]** It was Teddy with his hand on my leg, shaking me awake.

Stephen King, "The Body" (adapted)

PARAGRAPH FIVE

[ADD YOUR SENTENCE OF AT LEAST FORTY-FIVE WORDS.] On the floor, his scarred, bony head resting on one of the man's feet, lay an old white English bull terrier. His slanted almond-shaped eyes, sunk deep within their pinkish rims, were closed. **[ADD ANOTHER SENTENCE OF AT LEAST FIFTEEN WORDS.]**

He twitched and sighed often in his sleep, as old dogs will, and for once his shabby tail with the bare patch on the last joint was still. By the door lay another dog, nose on paws, brown eyes open and watchful in contrast to the peacefulness radiated by the other occupants of the room. **[ADD ANOTHER SENTENCE OF AT LEAST THIRTY WORDS.]**

Sheila Burnford, *The Incredible Journey*

ACTIVITY 5: EXPANDING PARAGRAPHS

In his sci-fi novel *The Martian Chronicles*, author Ray Bradbury wrote a paragraph describing a room full of "dead" robots, stored in coffinlike boxes, waiting to come "alive" again.

Here are the first few sentences of his paragraph, first without sentence-composing tools, next with sentence-composing tools in boldface:

WITHOUT SENTENCE-COMPOSING TOOLS

The roots waited. They waited. The robots waited. The robots lay. They waited to be set in motion.

WITH SENTENCE-COMPOSING TOOLS

Full grown without memory, the roots waited. **In green silks the color of forest pools, in silks the color of frog and fern,** they waited. In yellow hair the color of the sun and sand, the robots waited. **Oiled, with tube bones cut from bronze and sunk in gelatin,** the robots lay. **In coffins for the not dead and not alive, in planked boxes,** they waited to be set in motion.

The strength of Bradbury's paragraph results from his use of powerful sentence-composing tools that elaborate the scene and create suspense as the robots come "alive."

Directions: Following is the rest of Bradbury's paragraph, with sentence-composing tools removed. It ends when the robots, brought back to life, open their eyes. Partner with Bradbury by adding to Bradbury's sentences *at least three* powerful sentence-composing tools—any type, any place—and also by creating *at least three* well-built new sentences of your own.

(1) There was a smell of lubrication and lathed brass. (2) There was a silence of the tomb yard. (3) The robots waited. (4) The robots stared at the nailed lids of their wooden coffins. (5) Now there was a vast screaming of nails yanked out of the boxes. (6) Now there was a lifting of wooden lids. (7) Now there were robot shadows on the boxes and the pressure of a hand squirting oil from a can. (8) Now one robot was set in motion. (9) Now another and another arose. (10) Their marble eyes rolled wide their rubber lids.

BUILDING STRONGER PARAGRAPHS

Write a paragraph of *ten or more sentences*. Within, use sentence-composing tools of different types (*word*, *phrase*, *clause*) and lengths (*short*, *medium*, *long*) and places (*opener*, *S-V split*, *closer*). Like Bradbury's paragraph, yours should be highly interesting.

In your paragraph, imitate one of the model sentences from the list that follows. The rest of your sentences should be original, not imitations. All of the sentences in your paragraph should reflect maturity and variety. To achieve this blend, "bury" your imitation sentence within the paragraph so it doesn't stand out as better than the rest of your sentences.

MODEL SENTENCES
(Tools are **boldface**.)

1. **At the front of the room, facing the students**, was the desk of Mr. Porter.

   Jay Asher, *Thirteen Reasons Why*

2. Inside was the first beautiful thing I've seen in the District 13 compound, **a replication of a meadow, filled with real trees and flowering plants, and alive with hummingbirds.**

   Suzanne Collins, *Mockingjay*

3. **Sweet** and **clear**, it was like liquid sunlight, **better than anything he had ever had in his life.**

   Megan Whalen Turner, *The King of Attolia*

4. The old men smiled at me, **an English girl lost and alone on Bombay's streets**.

   Libba Bray, *A Great and Terrible Beauty*

5. As we passed an open doorway, a huge dog came bounding out, **snarling** and **barking at us.**

   Peter Abrahams, *Tell Freedom*

6. She made the local news, **speaking clearly and angrily to a local reporter, her eyes blazing, with half the school framed in the shot and cheering behind her.**

   Sarah Dessen, *Dreamland*

7. He was clambering heavily among the creepers and broken trunks, **when a bird, a vision of red and yellow, flashed upwards with a witch-like cry.**

   William Golding, *Lord of the Flies*

8. **Silent as the still water, quiet as one of the Indians from the lost tribes,** Clothilde moved through the trees.

Cynthia Voigt, *Tree by Leaf*

9. His father, **watching him, standing beside him,** started to cry.

Kate DiCamillo, *The Tiger Rising*

10. Her mother leaned forward, grasped her woolen jumper and jerked her back, **smacking her down with a sharp cuff.**

Elizabeth George Speare, *The Witch of Blackbird Pond*

Here are two versions of a paragraph containing an imitation of model 5 from the list, one poor, the other good. Compare them. Notice that the good version uses fewer sentences by condensing information and expressing it through a variety of sentence-composing tools.

EXAMPLE

- - - - - - - - - - - - - - - - - -

POOR: (*Imitation is very obvious.*)

Dance Class

(1) The students limbered up on the floor of the practice room. (2) They were preparing for this next lesson on popular dances. (3) The lesson tonight was going to be a variation on the three-step movement they learned last week. (4) (*imitation*) **When the instructor entered from the faculty room, the students began livening up, bouncing and swaying to the music.** (5) He entered without a word. (6) He was in deep concentration. (7) He walked over to the corner of the mirrored room to the music. (8) He switched the stereo off. (9) He then began dancing. (10) He danced without any music except the amazing rhythm of his moving body. (11) The only music was the rhythm of his fluent choreography. (12) The students were enthralled at his silent

steps. (13) The students stood staring. (14) Their feet started to tap out the rhythm in his motions. (15) Their fingers were snapping to his body's pulse. (16) The students were waiting for him to give the signal to let them join in.

GOOD: (*Imitation is not obvious.*)

Dance Class

(1) Limbering up on the floor of the practice room, the students prepared for their next lesson on popular dances, tonight a variation on the three-step movement they learned last week. (2) **(*imitation*)** **When the instructor entered from the faculty room, the students began livening up, bouncing and swaying to the music.** (3) Without a word, in deep concentration, he walked over to the corner of the mirrored room to the music, switched it off, and then began dancing, with no music except the amazing rhythm of his moving body, his fluent choreography. (4) Enthralled at his silent steps, the students stood staring, their feet starting to tap out the rhythm in his motions, fingers snapping to his body's pulse, waiting for him to give the signal to let them join in.

IMITATING PARAGRAPHS

Earlier, you learned to imitate sentences by authors. Imitating paragraphs by authors is similar. In this section, you will learn how the sentences in a model paragraph are built and then imitate that model paragraph, using your own topic but building your sentences like those in the model paragraph.

ACTIVITY 1: PARAGRAPH DESCRIBING AN ANIMAL

The model paragraph describes a terrifying junkyard dog named Chopper, which, according to legend, at his owner Milo's command would viciously attack any kids who tried to enter the junkyard. Read the model paragraph and the three paragraphs underneath it. Which two paragraphs imitate the sentence structures in the model paragraph?

To learn how the sentences in the model paragraph and the two imitation paragraphs are built alike, write out three equivalent sentences as a list: sentence number 1 from the model, plus the two sentences that imitate that sentence; sentence number 2 from the model, plus the two that imitate it, and so forth.

MODEL PARAGRAPH

(1) Ugly enough to stop a striking clock, Chopper was the most feared and meanest dog for forty miles around. (2) The kids whispered legends about Chopper's meanness. (3) The most common story was that Milo had trained Chopper not just to sic but to sic specific parts of the human anatomy. (4) An unfortunate kid who had illegally scaled the dump fence to pick up illicit treasure might hear Milo yell for Chopper to sic the kid's hand. (5) Chopper would grab that hand and hold on, ripping skin and tendons, powdering bones between his slavering jaws, until Milo told him to quit. (6) It was rumored that Chopper could take an ear, an eye, a foot, or a leg.

Stephen King, "The Body" (adapted)

QUESTIONS TO ANALYZE THE MODEL

1. What sentence contains an exaggeration?

2. What sentence begins with a sentence opener?

3. What sentence ends with three sentence closers?

PARAGRAPH ONE

(1) Kind enough to befriend a shrinking violet, Mrs. Sandstone was a most beloved and respected librarian in the central middle school. (2) Many students shared anecdotes about her kindness. (3) The most heartwarming story was that Mrs. Sandstone had chosen books not just to interest but to help each student with his or her personal problems. (4) A shy boy who had reluctantly walked into her welcoming library to pick up reading material might hear Mrs. Sandstone ask for the student to try a certain book. (5) The book would entrance the student and comfort him, touching heart and mind, healing hurts within its unfolding pages while Mrs. Sandstone nudged him to continue. (6) It was known that her favorite books could create a person, a place, an adventure, or an escape.

PARAGRAPH TWO

(1) Her face looked like a cracked ceramic vase, and, when in the presence of others, she was unable to show any warmth or any sympathy for anybody. (2) Worried, her family thought that she was probably beyond hope. (3) They all knew that she had once loved a man who had broken her heart into brittle pieces. (4) If anyone tried to talk to her about this tragic and unfortunate event, she would only lower her head, looking away. (5) You could almost see her reliving the event, as if it had just happened. (6) Her smile now gone forever and her laughter dried up, she was to be pitied.

PARAGRAPH THREE

       (1) Frightful enough to terrify a champion knight, Malvosio was the most loathsome and vengeful wizard in the entire kingdom. (2) The villagers shared warnings about Malvosio's evil. (3) The most bloodcurdling story was that Queen Zagarina had demanded Malvosio not just to punish but to kill innocent villagers for their weakening loyalty. (4) An unknowing farmer who had fearfully approached the wicked queen to ask for more land would hear the queen ask for Malvosio to torture the farmer's family. (5) Malvosio would find that family and punish them, speaking spells and curses, sprinkling venom over the entire family until the queen ordered him to stop. (6) It was understood that Malvosio could break a heart, an arm, a will, or a future.

ACTIVITY 2: IMITATING THE FIRST SENTENCE

Use or adapt one of the sentences that follow—or create your own—to use as the first sentence of a six-sentence paragraph that imitates the model paragraph by Stephen King (page 161).

Model Sentence: Ugly enough to stop a striking clock, Chopper was the most feared and meanest dog for forty miles around.

1. Brave enough to calm an attacking zombie, he was the most liked and neatest kid for blocks around.

2. Smart enough to explain a complex algebraic formula, she was the most gifted and talented student in math class.

3. Silent enough to evade an experienced trapper, the mink was the most beautiful and sought after animal in the entire country.

4. Beautiful enough to shame a blooming exotic orchid, she was the most memorable and envied girl in her high school.

5. Raucous enough to ruin any academic class, he was the most disruptive and difficult student in the entire school.

6. Passionate enough to begin her own political movement, she was the most intense and driven girl in her freshman class.

7. Experienced enough to handle any misbehaving child, she was the most popular and cherished babysitter for the entire neighborhood.

8. Serene enough to quell a burgeoning mutiny, the captain was the most calm and capable leader in the large fleet.

ACTIVITY 3: IMITATING THE REST OF THE SENTENCES

The sentences from the model paragraph are broken down into their sentence parts to help you focus on how each part is built. Imitate each sentence part, one at a time, to write sentences for your paragraph resembling the sentences in the model paragraph.

1a. Ugly enough

1b. to stop a striking clock,

1c. Chopper was the most feared

1d. and meanest dog for forty miles around.

2a. The kids whispered legends

2b. about Chopper's meanness.

3a. The most common story

3b. was that Milo had trained Chopper

3c. not just to sic

3d. but to sic specific parts

3e. of the human anatomy.

4a. An unfortunate kid

4b. who had illegally scaled the dump fence

4c. to pick up illicit treasure

4d. might hear Milo yell for Chopper

4e. to sic the kid's hand.

5a. Chopper would grab that hand and hold on,

5b. ripping skin and tendons,

5c. powdering bones between his slavering jaws,

5d. until Milo told him to quit.

6a. It was rumored

6b. that Chopper could take

6c. an ear, an eye, a foot, or a leg.

ASSIGNMENT FOR A PARAGRAPH DESCRIBING AN ANIMAL

Using the new model paragraph that follows, a description of a horse, describe a real or imagined animal by imitating the sentences in the model.

To simplify imitating its sentences, break each sentence down into a list of its parts, and then imitate one part at a time.

MODEL PARAGRAPH

(1) In the old school they use now for the village hall, below the clock that has stood always at one minute past ten, hangs a small dusty portrait of a horse. (2) He stands, a splendid red bay with a remarkable white cross emblazoned on his forehead and four perfectly matched white socks. (3) He looks wistfully out of the picture, his ears pricked forward, his head turned as if he has just noticed us standing there.

Michael Morpurgo, *War Horse*

ACTIVITY 4: PARAGRAPH DESCRIBING AN IMPORTANT EVENT

The model paragraph describes something that actually happened on an island in the Pacific Ocean: the most devastating volcanic eruption in history. Read the model paragraph and the three paragraphs underneath it. Which two paragraphs imitate the sentence structures in the model paragraph?

To learn how the sentences in the model paragraph and the two imitation paragraphs are built alike, write out three equivalent sentences as a list: sentence number 1 from the model, plus the two sentences that imitate that sentence; sentence number 2 from the model, plus the two that imitate it, and so forth.

MODEL PARAGRAPH

(1) There is a volcanic island named Krakatoa in the Pacific, and it blew up in 1883 with the biggest explosion of all time. (2) The sound of the explosion was heard for three thousand miles away, which is the greatest distance sound has ever been known to travel. (3) The violence

of the eruption caused dust, ashes, and stones to be hurled seventeen miles high into the air. (4) The black cloud of ejected material darkened an area with a radius of one hundred and fifty miles from the eruption. (5) Waves generated by the explosion reached a height of fifty feet, destroying countless vessels, swamping and inundating and completely destroying villages on islands hundreds of miles away, and causing thousands of casualties.

William Pène du Bois, *The Twenty-One Balloons* (adapted)

QUESTIONS TO ANALYZE THE MODEL

1. Which sentence is actually two sentences connected by a comma plus *and*?

2. What is the sentence-closer tool in sentence 2?

3. What sentence has a series of three sentence-closer tools of various lengths?

PARAGRAPH ONE

(1) About 230 miles northeast of Tokyo, the 2011 earthquake off the Pacific coast became known in the popular media coverage as the *tsunami*, which is the name for huge waves created by an earthquake underneath the water. (2) This great east Japan earthquake, biggest in Japan's history, triggered powerful tsunami waves that were up to 100 feet high, and which traveled up to six miles inland. (3) The tsunami compromised several nuclear reactors, with their cooling systems inoperable, and put the entire island on alert for evacuation. (4) The police reported 15,854 deaths, 6,000 injured, and over 3,000 people missing as well as thousands of buildings totally collapsed. (5) Entire villages were wiped out, leaving thousands of people homeless and making the aftermath look like a bomb had hit the island.

PARAGRAPH TWO

(1) It was a terrifying hurricane named Katrina in the Atlantic, and it arrived in 2005 as one of the deadliest hurricanes in United States history. (2) The flooding from the hurricane caused severe destruction from Texas to Louisiana, which was the greatest damage a hurricane in this country ever was recorded to cause. (3) The strength of the storm surge caused boats and casino barges to ram buildings and push cars and houses inland. (4) The catastrophic failure of the New Orleans levy system flooded 80 percent of the city and large tracks of outlying areas. (5) The worst damage from the hurricane affected Mississippi beachfront towns, flooding 90 percent of them in hours, sustaining damage from water that reached six to twelve miles inland, and costing eighty-one billion dollars and thousands of lives.

PARAGRAPH THREE

(1) There was a landing by Apollo 11 on the moon, and it happened on July 20, 1969, with Neil Armstrong and Buzz Aldren. (2) This United States mission is considered the major accomplishment in space exploration, which includes the most memorable footage ever taken on the moon. (3) The landing of the lunar module allowed fear, anxiety, and fantasy to be eradicated instantly in the TV audience's perception of the moon. (4) The successful landing of the lunar module on the face of the moon permitted Armstrong and Aldrin to spend twenty-one hours, thirty-one minutes on the lunar surface. (5) Success documented by this Apollo mission guaranteed six more missions to the moon, adding new information, eliminating and completely destroying images of science-fiction monsters on the moon, and inspiring astronauts of the future.

ACTIVITY 5: IMITATING THE FIRST SENTENCE

Use one of the sentences that follow about an important event—or create your own—to use as the first sentence of a five-sentence paragraph that imitates the model paragraph by William Pène du Bois (pages 166–167). First, get information for your paragraph by researching your topic online to learn details of the event for your paragraph.

> *Model Sentence:* There is a volcanic island named Krakatoa in the Pacific, and it blew up in 1883 with the biggest explosion of all time.

---

1. There was an Olympic athlete named Bruce Jenner in the 1970s, and he won the gold medal in the decathlon in the 1976 summer Olympics in Montreal.

2. There was a brilliant businessman named Steve Jobs in the computer industry, and he wound up with the most successful business of the twenty-first century.

3. There was a surprise attack on Pearl Harbor in the Pacific, and it began on December 7, 1941 with the Japanese unexpected air strikes on this United States island.

4. There was a brilliant scientist named Einstein in the late nineteenth and early twentieth centuries, and he caused a revolution in physics with the development of his theory of general relativity.

5. There was a plague named the "Black Death" in Europe, and it killed an estimated twenty-five million people or 30 to 60 percent of the European population at the time.

6. There was a fifty-six-game hitting streak from Joe DiMaggio of the New York Yankees, and it held up since 1941 as the unbeatable record of all time.

7. There was a tragic space shuttle explosion on the Challenger liftoff, and it killed all the astronauts within the first minutes of launch of the spacecraft.

8. There is a legendary story about Benjamin Franklin in 1752, and it sums up his discovery of the connection between lightning and electricity.

ACTIVITY 6: IMITATING THE REST OF THE SENTENCES

The sentences from the model paragraph are broken down into their sentence parts to help you focus on how each part is built. Imitate each sentence part, one at a time, to write sentences for your paragraph resembling the sentences in the model paragraph.

1a. There is a volcanic island named Krakatoa in the Pacific,

1b. and it blew up in 1883

1c. with the biggest explosion of all time.

2a. The sound of the explosion was heard

2b. as far as three thousand miles away,

2c. which is the greatest distance sound has ever been known to travel.

3a. The violence of the eruption caused

3b. dust, ashes, and stones

3c. to be hurled seventeen miles high into the air.

4a. The black cloud of ejected material

4b. darkened an area

4c. with a radius of one hundred and fifty miles from the eruption.

5a. Waves generated by the explosion

5b. reached a height of fifty feet,

5c. destroying countless vessels,

5d. swamping and inundating and completely destroying villages

5e. on islands hundreds of miles away,

5f. and causing thousands of casualties.

ASSIGNMENT FOR A PARAGRAPH DESCRIBING AN IMPORTANT EVENT

Choose one of these two topics: (1) events surrounding your own birth, or (2) circumstances of the attacks in the United States on September 11, 2001. For either, first research the topic to get details for the content of your paragraph: interviewing your parents if you are writing about your birth or searching online for details about 9/11.

Using the new model paragraph that follows, a description of the moment the atomic bomb went off on the Japanese city of Hiroshima, describe people associated with your birth or the events of 9/11 by imitating the sentences in the model. To simplify imitating its sentences, break each sentence down into a list of its parts, and then imitate one part at a time.

MODEL PARAGRAPH

(1) At exactly fifteen minutes past eight in the morning, on August 6, 1945, Japanese time, at the moment when the atomic bomb flashed above Hiroshima, Miss Toshiko Sasaki, a clerk in the personnel department of the East Asia Tin Works, had just sat down at her place in the plant office and was turning her head to speak to the girl at the next desk. (2) At that same moment, Dr. Masakazu Fujii was settling

down to read the newspaper on the porch of his hospital, overhanging one of the seven deltaic rivers that divide Hiroshima. (3) Mrs. Hatsuyu Nakamura, a tailor's widow, stood by the window of her kitchen, watching a neighbor tearing down his house because it was in the path of a fire lane. (4) Mr. Kiyoshi Tanimoto, the pastor of the Hiroshima Methodist Church, paused at the door of a rich man's house in Koi, the city's western suburb. (5) A hundred thousand people were killed by the bomb, and these people were among the survivors.

John Hersey, *Hiroshima* (adapted)

ACTIVITY 7: PARAGRAPH DESCRIBING A TERRIFYING EXPERIENCE

The model paragraph narrates a nightmarish scenario in which a boy on his bike is pursued by a would-be killer in a black car, holding a baseball bat as a murder weapon. Read the model paragraph and the three paragraphs that follow it. Identify two paragraphs that imitate the sentence structures in the model paragraph.

To learn how the sentences in the model paragraph and the two imitation paragraphs are built alike, write out three equivalent sentences as a list: sentence number 1 from the model, plus the two sentences that imitate that sentence; sentence number 2 from the model, plus the two that imitate it, and so forth.

MODEL PARAGRAPH

(1) Riding my bike, I heard a loud roar like an animal's, like a predator snarling. (2) I swiveled my head around, still pedaling, and looked back and saw it, a black car, just an outline at first, then clear and detailed. (3) I saw a man hanging out of the passenger window, hanging way out. (4) He had something pulled over his face, some kind of ski mask, and he was holding a long metal baseball bat in both hands, like

a murder weapon. (5) I swiveled back, terrified, and pedaled as hard as I could. (6) The man in the ski mask leaned farther out of the window and pulled the bat back and up. (7) Then he brought it forward in a mighty swing, aimed right at my head. (8) I dove to the right, landing on my face in the grass, just as the baseball bat smashed into the mailbox, exploding it right off its pole. (9) I scrambled back up, leaving my bike there, its wheels spinning, and ran for home. (10) I ran in absolute terror, listening for the sound of the car squealing back around to come after me again.

Edward Bloor, *Tangerine*

QUESTIONS TO ANALYZE THE MODEL

1. What two sentences contain comparisons beginning with like?

2. What words in the paragraph communicate the terror the bike rider felt?

3. Why is the final sentence terrifying?

4. Most sentences contain removable sentence parts, namely, various kinds of sentence-composing tools. Choose one of the sentences and jot down all removable sentence parts. How do those parts add power to the sentence?

PARAGRAPH ONE

(1) Looking out the window, I saw a blast of fire heading across the field, bringing smoke. (2) I raced to the kitchen, heading for the phone, and thought about somebody I could call, and somebody who would be able to help with this raging fiery menace, moving closer and closer. (3) I heard someone ringing a bell, frantically, intending to alert people

to the danger. (4) He was dressed totally in white fabric, which must have been fireproof, and he was running toward neighboring houses as he rang his bell. (5) I continued watching, hoping that some help would come to our rescue. (6) The man with the bell kept running, running, running, and calling the names of his neighbors. (7) Suddenly, he found himself on fire, his hands, like two torches, no longer useful. (8) I ran out my front door, my heart pounding in fright, my lungs filling with smoke, my courage beginning to dissipate as I approached the human torch. (9) I reached out toward him, slamming him down on the ground so that I could beat the flames with my coat. (10) With all my strength, I started beating, beating until most of the fire had been extinguished.

PARAGRAPH TWO

(1) Walking the path, I heard a soft rustle, like a breeze, like an animal moving. (2) I slowed my steps somewhat, still walking, and looked ahead and saw it, a large snake, just a blur at first, then moving and frightening. (3) I saw the fangs protruding out of the ugly mouth, protruding far out. (4) The snake had scales lined down its back, some sort of geometric pattern, and it was attacking a small furry rodent with those fangs like a hypodermic needle. (5) I stood still, frozen, and stared as quietly as possible. (6) The snake in the high grass stopped momentarily beside a rock and bit the rodent again and again. (7) Then he pushed it down in a terrifying swallow, gulped visibly down its body. (8) I backed up the path, treading on my feet in absolute silence, just as the snake again started its slinky movement, circling back in my direction. (9) I turned around then, lifting my legs quietly, my feet trembling, and moved toward safety. (10) I walked in an icy panic, listening for the sound of the snake coming back toward me to stalk me like the rodent.

PARAGRAPH THREE

(1) Walking the road, I heard a loud rush, like a flood, like a tsunami starting. (2) I turned my head around, still walking, and looked back and saw a huge wave, just a curl right now, then bigger and broader. (3) I saw several people submerged under the dark surface, submerged face down. (4) They had nothing protective over their bodies, no life preservers of any sort, and they were struggling many feet under the surface with no hope, like a water-logged mattress. (5) I looked back speechless and ran as fast as I could. (6) The bodies in the water moved closer to the oncoming victims and pushed their hands around and down. (7) Then the bodies washed toward me in a heavy mass under my arms. (8) I plunged under the water, diving underneath a submerged plank, just as the swirling bodies passed over my head, sending the corpses up the torrent. (9) I kicked to the surface, gasping for fresh air, my lungs bursting, and swam toward the vortex. (10) I kicked with frantic ferocity, hoping for a hint of some help reaching out toward me to extract me from the flood.

ACTIVITY 8: IMITATING THE FIRST SENTENCE

Choose one of the sentences that follow—or create your own—to use as the first sentence of a ten-sentence paragraph that imitates the model paragraph by Bloor (pages 172–173).

Model Sentence: Riding my bike, I heard a loud roar like an animal's, like a predator snarling.

1. Hearing downstairs footsteps, the child feared a terrifying monster like Dracula, like a vampire stalking.

2. Losing his balance, the swimmer felt a strong pull like a whirlpool, like a drain emptying.

3. Spotting something hairy, the camper swatted a moving insect like a spider, like a tarantula creeping.

4. Noticing a funnel cloud, we gathered the children like a parent, like a mom protecting.

5. Nearing their raft, Emilio spotted a dark object like a wedge, like a shark circling.

6. Opening the garage, the detective smelled a rancid odor like a corpse's, like garbage rotting.

7. Closing his eyes, the kid saw a ghostly shape like a cloud, like a phantom prowling.

8. Nearing his tent, Cranston sensed a moving presence like a predator, like a bear scavenging.

ACTIVITY 9: IMITATING THE REST OF THE SENTENCES

The sentences from the model paragraph are broken down into their sentence parts to help you focus on how each part is built. Imitate each sentence part, one at a time, to write sentences for your paragraph resembling the sentences in the model paragraph.

1a. Riding my bike,

1b. I heard a loud roar

1c. like an animal's,

1d. like a predator snarling.

2a. I swiveled my head around,

2b. still pedaling,

2c. and looked back

2d. and saw it,

2e. a black car,

2f. just an outline at first,

2g. then clear and detailed.

3a. I saw a man hanging out of the passenger window,

3b. hanging way out.

4a. He had something pulled over his face,

4b. some kind of ski mask,

4c. and he was holding a long metal baseball bat in both hands,

4d. like a murder weapon.

5a. I swiveled back,

5b. terrified,

5c. and pedaled

5d. as hard as I could.

6a. The man in the ski mask leaned farther out of the window

6b. and pulled the bat back and up.

7a. Then he brought it forward in a mighty swing,

7b. aimed right at my head.

8a. I dove to the right,

8b. landing on my face in the grass,

8c. just as the baseball bat smashed into the mailbox,

8d. exploding it right off its pole.

9a. I scrambled back up,

9b. leaving my bike there,

9c. its wheels spinning,

9d. and ran for home.

10a. I ran in absolute terror,

10b. listening for the sound of the car squealing back around

10d. to come after me again.

ASSIGNMENT FOR A PARAGRAPH DESCRIBING A TERRIFYING EXPERIENCE

Using the new model paragraph that follows, a description of an excruciatingly painful medical procedure on a young boy named Ender, describe a real or imagined terrifying experience by imitating the sentences in the model. To simplify imitating its sentences, break each sentence down into a list of its parts, and then imitate one part at a time.

MODEL PARAGRAPH

(1) The doctor was twisting something at the back of Ender's head. (2) Suddenly a pain stabbed through him like a needle from his neck to his groin. (3) Ender felt his back spasm, and his body arched violently backward, his head striking the bed. (4) He could feel his legs thrashing, and his hands were clenching each other, wringing each other so tightly that they ached.

Orson Scott Card, *Ender's Game*

ACTIVITY 10: IMITATING AN OPENING PARAGRAPH

Written by recognizable authors, the model paragraphs that follow are the opening paragraphs of stories. Write just the opening paragraph of a story, although you may want to finish it later. Study the model paragraphs to learn how the authors attract the attention of readers, and then choose one model to imitate for an opening paragraph of a story.

MODEL PARAGRAPH ONE

(1) I clasped the flask between my hands even though the warmth from the tea had long since leached into the frozen air. (2) My muscles were clenched tight against the cold. (3) If a pack of wild dogs were to appear at this moment, the odds of scaling a tree before they attacked were not in my favor. (4) I should have got up, moved around, and worked the stiffness from my limbs. (5) Instead I sat, as motionless as the rock beneath me, while the dawn began to lighten the woods. (6) I couldn't fight the sun. (7) I could only watch helplessly as it dragged me into a day that I've been dreading for months.

Suzanne Collins, *Catching Fire* (adapted)

MODEL PARAGRAPH TWO

(1) He waited on the stoop until twilight, pretending to watch the sun melt into the dirty gray Harlem sky. (2) Up and down the street, car stereos were on and blared into the sour air. (3) Men dragged out card tables, laughing. (4) Cars cruised through the garbage and broken glass, older guys showing off their Friday night girls.

Robert Lipsyte, *The Contender*

MODEL PARAGRAPH THREE

(1) In a hole in the ground there lived a hobbit, not a nasty, dirty, wet hole, filled with the ends of worms and an oozy smell, nor yet a dry, bare, sandy hole with nothing in it to sit down on or to eat. (2) It was a hobbit-hole, and that means comfort. (3) It had a perfectly round door like a porthole, painted green, with a shiny yellow brass knob in the exact middle. (4) The door opened on to a tube-shaped hall like a tunnel, a very comfortable tunnel without smoke, with paneled walls, and floors tiled and carpeted, provided with polished chairs, and lots and lots of pegs for hats and coats because the hobbit was fond of visitors.

J. R. R. Tolkien, *The Hobbit*

MODEL PARAGRAPH FOUR

(1) Mr. Jones, of the Manor Farm, had locked the hen-houses for the night, but was too drunk to remember to shut the pop-holes. (2) With the ring of light from his lantern dancing from side to side, he lurched across the yard, kicked off his boots at the back door, drew himself a last glass of beer from the barrel in the scullery, and made his way to bed, where Mrs. Jones was already snoring.

George Orwell, *Animal Farm*

MODEL PARAGRAPH FIVE

My mother drove me to the airport with the windows rolled down. It was seventy-five degrees in Phoenix, the sky a perfect, cloudless blue. I was wearing my favorite shirt, sleeveless, white eyelet lace. I was wearing it as a farewell gesture. My carry-on item was a parka.

Stephenie Meyer, *Twilight*

In the scrambled paragraph that follows, sentence parts and sentences are out of order. Readers, confused, only know that the paragraph says something about a monster. In the unscrambled version, sentence parts and sentences are in order, and readers can easily understand the paragraph.

SCRAMBLED PARAGRAPH

(1) To glow like barbecue coals her eyes began. (2) A shriveled hag with big wings and claws she was and full of yellow fangs a mouth, and about to slice me to ribbons she was. (3) Wasn't human she. (4) Melted into large, leathery wings her jacket. (5) Turning into talons, her fingers stretched. (6) Happened the weirdest thing.

UNSCRAMBLED PARAGRAPH

(1) The weirdest thing happened. (2) Her eyes began to glow like barbecue coals. (3) Her fingers stretched, turning into talons. (4) Her jacket melted into large, leathery wings. (5) She wasn't human. (6) She was a shriveled hag with big wings and claws and a mouth full of yellow fangs, and she was about to slice me to ribbons.

Rick Riordan, *The Lightning Thief*

The two versions have exactly the same words, but the scrambled version is almost meaningless, a jumble of words, while the unscrambled version is meaningful, a description of a horrible transformation of a woman into a menacing birdlike monster.

In good sentences, like those in the unscrambled version, sentence parts have a clear relationship to each other. In good paragraphs, sentences also have a clear relationship to each other. These activities focus on those clear relationships of sentence parts within sentences, and sentences within paragraphs.

Zoom in now on how to achieve clear relationships within and among a paragraph's sentences.

ACTIVITY 1: NARRATIVE PARAGRAPH

A narrative paragraph tells either a true or a fictional story. Each list that follows, when unscrambled, will become one of the sentences in a narrative paragraph from Larry McMurtry's novel *Lonesome Dove*. In McMurtry's paragraph, the main character Augustus steps out onto a porch and sees two pigs eating a rattlesnake.

Unscramble and punctuate the lists to produce the four sentences in the paragraph. In each list, the sentence part that begins the sentence is capitalized.

Important: Type or write out the list of four unscrambled sentences from the following activity. In the next activity, you need that list to arrange the sentences into a meaningful paragraph.

1a. by the neck

1b. and the shoat had the tail

1c. The sow had it

2a. when it ran into the pigs

2b. just been crawling around

2c. It had probably

2d. looking for shade

3a. on the porch

3b. not a very big one

6a. the sea has been an area of unrest

6b. All through the long history of Earth

6c. and where the tides have receded, and then returned

6d. where waves have broken heavily against the land

The six unscrambled sentences are not in the order of the original paragraph, so arrange them in a way that makes the most sense. Write out and punctuate the paragraph.

ASSIGNMENT FOR INFORMATIVE PARAGRAPH

Write an informative paragraph about how storms happen: for example, a tornado, a hurricane, a lightning strike, a tsunami, or some other devastating natural event. Research your topic before drafting your paragraph to learn more about that particular kind of storm.

ACTIVITY 3: PROCESS PARAGRAPH

A process paragraph describes how something occurs. Each list that follows, when unscrambled, will become one of the sentences in a paragraph from William Pène du Bois' award-winning story *The Twenty-One Balloons*. In his whimsical paragraph, the author explains how traveling in a balloon to school can be delightful.

Unscramble and punctuate the lists to produce the seven sentences in the paragraph. In each list, the sentence part that begins the sentence is capitalized.

Important: Type or write out the list of seven unscrambled sentences from the following activity. In the next activity, you need that list to arrange the sentences into a meaningful paragraph.

1a. can happen

1b. On your way

1c. many delightful things

2a. climb into the basket

2b. untie the ropes

2c. You get up early in the morning with your school-books

2d. look in the direction of the school building

2e. and fly off

3a. just once

3b. and take you fifty miles out into the country

3c. The wind will blow you in the wrong direction

3d. away from school

3e. and nobody can bother you in a balloon

3f. and you might decide to play hookey

4a. and you'll never get to school

4b. will be calm

4c. The wind

5a. is the best

5b. particularly between home and school

5c. Balloon travel

6a. from your home to school

6b. In a balloon

6c. particularly if you want to travel

6d. is a wonderful way to travel

7a. and change your mind

7b. onto the roof of the grandstand

7c. Then, too

7d. you might fly over a ball park on the way

7e. as you make a quick descent

7f. you can drop a line and do some fine fishing

7g. or if you pass any lakes on the way to school

The seven unscrambled sentences are not in the order of the original paragraph, so arrange them in a way that makes the most sense. Write out and punctuate the paragraph.

ASSIGNMENT FOR A PROCESS PARAGRAPH

Describe a fantasy process, like the one in the model paragraph, or, if you prefer, a real process. If you choose a fantasy process, use your imagination to explain it. If you choose a real process, first research that process to learn more about how it works. End your paragraph with a sentence that emphasizes the importance of the process you've described.

ACTIVITY 4: DESCRIPTIVE PARAGRAPH

A descriptive paragraph creates a movie in the reader's mind. Each list that follows, when unscrambled, will become one of the sentences in a descriptive paragraph from Neil Gaiman's novel *The Graveyard Book*. In Gaiman's paragraph, the narrator describes a particular grave, where a ghoul lurks.

Unscramble and punctuate the lists to produce the six sentences in the paragraph. In each list, the sentence part that begins the sentence is capitalized.

Important: Type or write out the list of six unscrambled sentences from the activity that follows. In the next activity, you need that list to arrange the sentences into a meaningful paragraph.

1a. is all too often impossible to read

1b. than other gravestones, too

1c. and the name on the stone

1d. It may be colder

2a. or so scabbed with fungus and lichens

2b. If there is a statue on the grave

2c. as to look like a fungus itself

2d. it will be headless

3a. is one

3b. in every graveyard

3c. There

4a. belongs to the ghouls

4b. in every graveyard

4c. One grave

5a. that is the ghoul-gate

5b. want to be somewhere else

5c. If the grave makes you

6a. and a feeling when you reach it of abandonment

6b. water-stained and bulging

6c. Wander any graveyard long enough

6d. with cracked or broken stone, scraggly grass or rank weeds about it

6e. and you will find it

The six unscrambled sentences are not in the order of the original paragraph, so arrange them in a way that makes the most sense. Write out and punctuate the paragraph.

ASSIGNMENT FOR DESCRIPTIVE PARAGRAPH

Write a descriptive paragraph about an unusual place: a junkyard, an overgrown lot, an abandoned house, an alley, or someplace else. Begin your paragraph with a sentence that previews the place, as in the model. Describe all the details that make the place unusual. Also, end your paragraph with a sentence that summarizes the paragraph, as in the model.

ACTIVITY 5: EXPLANATORY PARAGRAPH

An explanatory paragraph explains an idea or fact, often through illustrations. Each list that follows, when unscrambled, will become one of the sentences in an explanatory paragraph from Jacqueline Kelly's *The Evolution of Calpurnia Tate*. The paragraph applies Darwin's theory of the survival of the fittest to explain why certain grasshoppers are eaten by birds, but others are not.

Unscramble and punctuate the lists to produce the five sentences in the paragraph. In each list, the sentence part that begins the sentence is capitalized.

Important: Type or write out the list of five unscrambled sentences from the activity that follows. In the next activity, you need that list to arrange the sentences into a meaningful paragraph.

1a. the ones the birds pick off

1b. to grow big

1c. The greener ones

1d. don't last long enough

2a. gobbling them up

2b. hide nearby

2c. and taunt their less-fortunate brothers

2d. The birds spend their days

2e. while the yellow grasshoppers

3a. because they are more fit to survive

3b. hidden by the parched yellowed grass

3c. Only the yellower ones survive

3d. in the torrid weather

4a. to spot

4b. are just too easy

4c. The bright green grasshoppers

5a. that are born a bit yellower

5b. The grasshoppers

5c. to begin with

5d. because the birds can't see them

5e. live to an old age in the drought

5f. in the parched grass

The five unscrambled sentences are not in the order of the original paragraph, so arrange them in a way that makes the most sense. Write out and punctuate the paragraph.

ASSIGNMENT FOR EXPLANATORY PARAGRAPH

Write an explanatory paragraph about something in nature: light in a lightning bug, transformation of a caterpillar into a butterfly, change of leaf color in the fall, emergence of flowers from bulbs in the spring, or something else. First research that process to learn more about how it works. Finish the paragraph with a sentence summarizing the explanation.

Sentences are the bricks as well as the mortar,
the motor as well as the fuel.
One in front of the other marks the way.

—Jhumpa Lahiri, "My Life Sentences"

BUILDING PARAGRAPHS

The best cars have lots of extras to attract buyers, additions like great sound systems, stunning wheels, leather seats, and so forth. The best paragraphs, and the sentences they contain, also have extras to attract readers, sentence parts and sentences that add useful details and information. Accessories are to cars what elaboration is to writing. For cars or for paragraphs, additions make a much better product. In these final activities, you'll use sentence-composing tools you've learned for those additions to paragraphs.

ACTIVITY 1: PLACING ADDITIONS

Throughout the activities in *Paragraphs for Middle School: A Sentence-Composing Approach*, you learned repeatedly that additions build better paragraphs, and you practiced using sentence-composing tools for those additions. Underneath each sentence of the paragraph are additions that appear in the author's original paragraph. Insert the additions where they are most effective, punctuating them with commas where needed. **Note:** *The additions are scrambled, not in the order they appear in the original paragraph. Insert them where they make the most sense.*

PARAGRAPH ONE

from *The Wonderful Wizard of Oz* by L. Frank Baum—Dorothy, stuck in the land of Oz, yearning to return to her home in Kansas, realizes sadly that going home will be very difficult.

1. Dorothy's life became very sad.
   a. that it would be harder than ever
   b. as she grew to understand
   c. to get back to Kansas and Aunt Em again

2. She would cry bitterly for hours.

   a. to show how sorry he was for his little mistress

   b. and looking into her face

   c. Toto sitting at her feet

   d. whining dismally

3. Toto did not really care whether he was in Kansas or the Land of Oz, but the dog knew the little girl was unhappy.

   a. making him unhappy, too

   b. if Dorothy was with him

PARAGRAPH TWO

from *Beatrice and Virgil* by Yann Martel—A trio of tigers stuffed by a taxidermist is described.

1. A male was crouching.

   a. every hair bristling

   b. staring dead ahead

   c. ears swiveled around

2. A female stood a little behind him.

   a. her tail anxiously curled in the air

   b. a paw raised in the air

   c. a snarl upon her face

3. A cub had his head turned to one side, but he too was apprehensive.

   a. lastly

   b. his claws drawn

   c. distracted momentarily

PARAGRAPH THREE

from *Watership Down* by Richard Adams—To explore for food, several rabbits leave their holes.

1. The dry slope was dotted with rabbits.
   a. that the rest had missed
   b. some nibbling at the thin grass near their holes
   c. a delicacy among rabbits
   d. others pushing further down to look for dandelions or perhaps a cowslip

2. One sat upright on an ant heap and looked about.
   a. and nose in the wind
   b. here and there
   c. with ears erect

3. A blackbird showed that there was nothing alarming there, and in the other direction, all was plain to be seen.
   a. with the warren at peace
   b. singing undisturbed on the outskirts of the wood
   c. empty and quiet
   d. along the brook

PARAGRAPH FOUR

from *Cat's Table* by Michael Ondaatje—Eleven-year-old Michael recalls a traveling circus on a road in a forest.

1. Then the sound of a fanfare emerged.
   a. some more magically from the high branches of the trees
   b. some of it out of the depths of the forest
   c. where the trumpeter was

2. A man seemingly on fire swept down on a rope.
   a. catching another rope
   b. smoke trailing behind him
   c. along the stretch of audience-covered road
   d. skimming the spectators' heads
   e. and swinging this way further and further
   f. his face painted like a bird's

3. Then the rest of the acrobats came out, and for the next hour leapt from trees into the empty air and were caught in the arms of others.
   a. who seemed to fall from even greater heights
   b. in stained and ragged colors

4. Men walked across tightropes stretched from tree to tree.
   a. carrying brimming buckets of water
   b. and hanging on with just one arm
   c. releasing the contents into the crowd
   d. slipping in mid-air

PARAGRAPH FIVE

from *Hatchet* by Gary Paulsen—Flying in a small plane, a young boy named Brian is forced to try to land the plane after the pilot has a fatal heart attack.

1. There was a great wrenching.
   a. ripping back just outside the plane's main braces
   b. as the plane's wings caught the pines at the side of the clearing and broke back

2. Brian thought there must have been some kind of explosion.
   a. dust and dirt blowing off the floor
   b. into his face so hard

3. He was momentarily blind.
   a. smashing his head on the wheel
   b. slammed forward in his seat

4. The plane rolled to the right and blew through the trees.
   a. water that drove him back into the seat
   b. skip once on water as hard as concrete
   c. after a wild crashing sound and ripping of metal
   d. out over the water and down
   e. water that tore the plane's windshield out and shattered the side windows
   f. down to slam in to the lake

5. Somebody was yelling, and Brian did not know that it was his sound.

   a. down in the water

   b. screaming as the plane dove down into the water

   c. that he roared against the water that took him and the plane still deeper

   d. screaming tight animal sounds of fear and pain

ACTIVITY 2: CREATING ADDITIONS

In the following paragraphs, additions have been removed. By using the sentence-composing tools you've learned, add sentence parts to build a much better paragraph. The number of words in the basic paragraph and the number of words in the original paragraph are provided. In your additions, approximate the number of words in the original paragraph.

EXAMPLE

Basic Paragraph

(1) He scanned his surroundings. (2) Golden hills rolled inland. (3) The flatlands of Berkeley and Oakland marched west. (4) San Francisco Bay glittered under a silvery haze. (5) A wall of fog had swallowed most of San Francisco.

Original Paragraph (*The author's additions are bolded.*)

(1) He scanned his surroundings. (2) **To his left**, golden hills rolled inland, **dotted with lakes, woods, and a few herds of cows.** (3) **To his right**, the flatlands of Berkeley and Oakland marched west—**a vast checkerboard of neighborhoods, with several million people who probably did not want their morning interrupted by two monsters and a filthy demigod.** (4) **Farther west**, San Francisco Bay glittered under a silvery haze. (5) **Past that**, a wall of fog had swallowed most of

San Francisco, **leaving just the tops of skyscrapers and towers of the Golden Gate Bridge**.

Rick Riordan, *Heroes of Olympus*

Note: *The basic paragraph has thirty-four words; the original paragraph ninety-one words,* **with almost 63 percent of the original being additions**.

PARAGRAPH ONE: A RUN AND A FALL

Basic Paragraph

(1) He ran blindly down the mountain path. (2) Several times he fell, but was on his feet again in the next breath. (3) He fell hard onto his face. (4) His teeth cut into his top lip, and he spat blood.

Linda Sue Park, *A Single Shard*

Note: *The basic paragraph has thirty-eight words; the original paragraph sixty-nine words,* **with almost 46 percent additions**.

PARAGRAPH TWO: A FAMILY FEAST

Basic Paragraph

(1) The children were astonished by the ham that their mother Kathleen had cooked. (2) It was the largest they had ever seen. (3) It was covered in a crust of brown sugar and molasses. (4) Buddy the Dog sat at attention. (5) Kathleen shooed him with a kick in the ribs, but he just let out a yelp and stayed put. (6) Russell the Cat came into the room, too, and sat facing the wall. (7) Their father Howard had specially sharpened the carving knife for the occasion. (8) He stood and leaned over the ham, and grinned at the children and at his wife. (9) Howard sliced into the ham.

Paul Harding, *Tinkers*

Note: *The basic paragraph has 103 words; the original paragraph 189 words,* **with 45 percent additions.**

PARAGRAPH THREE: GANDALF THE WIZARD

Basic Paragraph

(1) Gandalf came by. (2) If you had heard only a quarter of what I have heard about Gandalf, you would be prepared for any sort of remarkable tale. (3) Tales and adventures sprouted up all over the place wherever he went. (4) He had not been down that way for ages and ages, so the hobbits had almost forgotten what he looked like. (5) Gandalf for years had been away on businesses of his own. (6) All that Bilbo saw that morning was an old man with a staff.

J. R. R. Tolkien, *The Hobbit*

Note: *The basic paragraph has 84 words; the original paragraph 196 words,* **with 57 percent additions.**

PARAGRAPH FOUR: A CHILDHOOD PET REMEMBERED

Basic Paragraph

(1) I came across a faded photograph of my dog Skip not long ago. (2) I would admit I still missed him.

Willie Morris, *My Dog Skip*

Note: *The basic paragraph has twenty words; the original paragraph sixty-one words,* **with 67 percent additions.**

PARAGRAPH FIVE: A DILAPIDATED HOUSE FOR A POOR FAMILY

Basic Paragraph

(1) Here was a long, rickety house. (2) Here was a porch. (3) Here was a dirt yard. (4) Here were some out-buildings. (5) Here was our new home.

Hillary Jordan, *Mudbound*

Note: *The basic paragraph has twenty-four words; the original paragraph ninety-four words,* **with 75 percent additions**.

BUILDING STRONGER PARAGRAPHS

In their paragraphs, authors use additions to increase interest, content, and style. In the following paragraph, a poisonous snake in Fred Gipson's *Old Yeller* fails to bite a young boy's father, but then does bite the boy's dog.

Contrast the following versions of the paragraph, the first without tools, and the second (the original) with tools. The author uses additions in a variety of places. Notice their power.

WITHOUT ADDITIONS

(1) The snake bite happened. (2) A big diamond-back rattler struck at Papa. (3) Papa chopped his head off. (4) The head suddenly dropped to the ground three or four feet away from the writhing body. (5) It lay there. (6) Our dog went up and nuzzled that rattler's head. (7) He was falling back. (8) That snake mouth had snapped shut on his nose. (9) He died that night, and I cried for a week.

WITH ADDITIONS

The Snake

(1) The snake bite happened **while Papa and I were cutting wild hay in a little patch of prairie back of the house**. (2) A big diamond-back rattler, **near the wood pile**, struck at Papa. (3) **With one quick lick of his scythe**, Papa chopped his head off. (4) **Dangling**, the head suddenly dropped to the ground three or four feet away from the writhing body. (5) It lay there, **the ugly mouth opening and shutting, still trying to bite something**. (6) Our dog, **curious**, went up and nuzzled that rattler's head. (7) **A second later**, he was falling back, **howling** and **slinging his own head till his ears popped**. (8) That snake mouth had snapped shut on his nose, **driving the fangs in so deep that it was a full minute before he could sling the bloody head loose**. (9) He died that night, and I cried for a week.

OPENERS

- with one quick lick of his scythe
- dangling
- a second later

S-V SPLITS

- near the wood pile
- curious

CLOSERS

- while Papa and I were cutting wild hay in a little patch of prairie back of the house

- the ugly mouth opening and shutting, still trying to bite something

- howling

- slinging his own head till his ears popped

Now it's your turn. The following paragraph is based upon an incident in Cynthia Kadohata's story *Kira-Kira*, in which a dog attacks two children. In the following version, the author's additions have been removed.

For *at least five* sentences in the paragraph, create additions to make the paragraph even more terrifying. For your additions, choose places that work best—opener, S-V split, closer, or a mix.

The Ferocious Attack

(1) The dog burst from the field suddenly. (2) Its teeth were long and yellow. (3) The dog grabbed at my pants. (4) The dog ripped my pants and his cold teeth touched my skin. (5) Lynn pulled at the dog's tail and shouted at me to run. (6) I ran. (7) I turned around and saw the dog tearing at Lynn's pants. (8) I ran inside and looked for a weapon. (9) I got a milk bottle out of the fridge and ran toward Lynn and threw the bottle at the dog. (10) The bottle missed the dog and broke on the street. (11) The dog rushed to lap up the milk. (12) Lynn and I ran toward the house, but she stopped on the porch. (13) She got the water hose and chased the dog away with the water, so it wouldn't hurt its tongue. **[ADD TWO MORE SPECTACULAR, TERRIFYING SENTENCES! PUT YOUR SENTENCES ANYWHERE IN THE PARAGRAPH.]**

TOOLS FOR BETTER WRITING

Authors have always used the kind of tools you have learned in *Paragraphs for Middle School: A Sentence-Composing Approach* because those tools add power to writing. Following is a final example proving that point.

The Call of the Wild by Jack London tells the story of the dog Buck, who transforms from a domesticated dog to a sled dog in the Yukon, struggling to survive cruel treatment from humans, other dogs, and harsh freezing weather. In the following paragraph, Buck, in a wooden crate, is tormented and then mercilessly beaten with a club by a man in a red sweater after opening the entrance to the cage. The paragraph is presented without tools, then the original paragraph with tools restored.

PARAGRAPH WITHOUT TOOLS

(1) Buck was truly a red-eyed devil. (2) Straight at the man he launched his one hundred and forty pounds of fury. (3) Buck received a shock that checked his body. (4) He whirled over. (5) He had never been struck by a club in his life, and did not understand. (6) He was again on his feet. (7) Again the shock came, and he was brought crushingly to the ground. (8) This time he was aware that it was the club, but his madness knew no caution. (9) A dozen times he charged, and as often the club broke the charge. (10) He crawled to his feet. (11) He staggered limply about.

PARAGRAPH WITH TOOLS

(1) Buck was truly a red-eyed devil, **as he drew himself together for the spring, hair bristling, mouth foaming, a mad glitter in his blood-shot eyes.** (2) Straight at the man he launched his one hundred and forty pounds of fury, **surcharged with the pent passion of two**

days and nights. (3) **In mid air, just as his jaws were about to close on the man,** Buck received a shock that checked his body, **bringing his teeth together with an agonizing clip.** (4) He whirled over, **fetching the ground on his back and side.** (5) He had never been struck by a club in his life, and did not understand. (6) **With a snarl that was part bark and more scream,** he was again on his feet, **launching into the air.** (7) Again the shock came, and he was brought crushingly to the ground. (8) This time he was aware that it was the club, but his madness knew no caution. (9) A dozen times he charged, and as often the club broke the charge, **smashing him down.** (10) **After a particularly fierce blow,** he crawled to his feet, **too dazed to rush.** (11) He staggered limply about, **the blood flowing from nose and mouth and ears, his beautiful coat sprayed and flecked with bloody slaver.**

Writing unfolds one sentence at a time, one paragraph at a time. What makes a powerful paragraph? Paragraph power comes from sentence power. Then, now, and always, sentence-composing tools build good sentences and, because of them, good paragraphs.

In language, there is probably nothing better than to write or to read a good sentence or paragraph.

With all the authors' good sentences and paragraphs you've read, studied, and practiced throughout *Paragraphs for Middle School: A Sentence-Composing Approach*, now you can always kindle your creative spark to write powerful paragraphs like those by authors.

Author of the Inheritance series of fantasy novels, Christopher Paolini at age fifteen began writing *Eragon*, the first in the series, with a single sentence: "Wind howled through the night, carrying a scent that would change the world." That novel tells the engrossing story of a young farm boy and his dragon and their adventures.

Jack London wrote in the nineteenth century; Christopher Paolini, the twenty-first century. Then, now, and always, good writing reflects the kind of sentence-composing and paragraph-building skills you've learned.

On the following pages are over four hundred more authors, your invisible teachers in *Paragraphs for Middle School: A Sentence-Composing Approach*. Their writing illustrates the timelessness of those tools.

YOUR INVISIBLE TEACHERS

Over four hundred sources from literature are the basis for the activities in *Paragraphs for Middle School: A Sentence-Composing Approach*. Included are model sentences and paragraphs from hundreds of authors—your silent mentors, your invisible teachers.

- -

Writers learn to write by paying a certain sort of attention to the works of their great and less great predecessors in the medium of written language, as well as by merely reading them.

—Toni Cade Bambara, writer

- -

Alexander Gordon Smith, *Lockdown*
Alexander Key, *The Forgotten Door*
Alexander Petrunkevitch, "The Spider and the Wasp"
Alice Walker, *In Search of Our Mothers' Gardens*
Ann Brashares, *Girls in Pants*
Annie Dillard, *An American Childhood*
———, "Death of a Moth"
Ann Patchett, *Bel Canto*
Annie Dillard, "Death of a Moth"
Annie Proulx, "The Indian Wars Refought"
Antoine de Saint-Exupéry, *The Little Prince*
Anton Chekov, "The Bet"
Armstrong Sperry, *Call It Courage*
Avi, *Crispin: The Cross of Lead*
Barack Obama, *Dreams from My Father*
Barbara Kingsolver, *Pigs in Heaven*
Betsy Byars, *The Summer of the Swans*
Betty Smith, *A Tree Grows in Brooklyn*

Beverly Cleary, *Ramona and Her Father*
Bill Brittain, *The Wish Giver*
Bill and Vera Cleaver, *Where the Lilies Bloom*
Brian Selznick, *The Invention of Hugo Cabret*
C. S. Lewis, *The Chronicles of Narnia*
Carl Henry Rathjen, "Runaway Rig"
Carl Hiaasen, *Hoot*
Carolyn Keene, *Nancy Drew: The Bungalow Mystery*
Carrie Ryan, *The Forest of Hands and Teeth*
Cassandra Clare, *City of Bones*
Charles Dickens, *David Copperfield*
Charles R. Joy, "Hindu Girl of Surinam"
Christopher Paolini, *Eragon*
Clare Vanderpool, *Moon Over Manifest*
Claudia Gray, *Evernight*
Cynthia Kadohata, *Kira-Kira*
Cynthia Voigt, *Dicey's Song*
———, *Seventeen Against the Dealer*
———, *Tree by Leaf*
Daniel Keyes, "Flowers for Algernon"
Daphne du Maurier, "The Birds"
Diana Wynne Jones, *Howl's Moving Castle*
Diane Ackerman, "The Face of Beauty"
———, *The Zookeeper's Wife*
Donald M. Murray, "The Maker's Eye: Revising Your Own Manuscripts"
Dorothy M. Johnson, *The Day the Sun Came Out*
E. B. White, *Charlotte's Web*
E. L. Konigsburg, *The View from Saturday*
Edward Bloor, *Tangerine*
Eleanor Coerr, *Sadako and the Thousand Paper Cranes*
Elinor Mordaunt, "The Prince and the Goose Girl"
Elizabeth Bowen, "Foothold"
Elizabeth Coatsworth, "The Story of Wang Li"

Elizabeth George Speare, *The Witch of Blackbird Pond*

Ellen Raskin, *The Westing Game*

Eoin Colfer, *Artemis Fowl*

Eric Larson, *The Devil in the White City*

Ernest Hemingway, *A Farewell to Arms*

F. R. Buckley, "Gold-Mounted Guns"

Fanny Billingsley, *Chime*

Frances Hodgson Burnett, *The Secret Garden*

Frank O'Connor, "First Confession"

Franklin W. Dixon, *The Hardy Boys: The House on the Cliff*

Fred Gipson, *Old Yeller*

Fritz Leiber, "A Bad Day for Sales"

Garth Nix, *Sabriel*

Gary Paulsen, *Brian's Winter*

———, *Hatchet*

———, *The River*

Gaston Leroux, *The Phantom of the Opera*

Gene Olson, *The Roaring Road*

George Orwell, *Animal Farm*

George R. R. Martin, *A Game of Thrones*

Gina Berriault, "The Stone Boy"

Greg Mortenson, *Three Cups of Tea*

Hal Borland, *When the Legends Die*

Harper Lee, *To Kill a Mockingbird*

Helen Hunt Jackson, *Ramona*

Hillary Jordan, *Mudbound*

Holly Goldberg Sloan, *I'll Be There*

Howard Pyle, *Men of Iron*

Ingrid Law, *Savvy*

J. D. Salinger, *The Catcher in the Rye*

———, "For Esme—with Love and Squalor"

———, *Franny and Zooey*

———, "A Perfect Day for Bananafish"

J. K. Rowling, *Harry Potter and the Chamber of Secrets*

————, *Harry Potter and the Goblet of Fire*

————, *Harry Potter and the Prisoner of Azkaban*

————, *Harry Potter and the Sorcerer's Stone*

J. M. Coetzee, *Life and Times of Michael K*

J. R. R. Tolkien, *The Hobbit*

Jack London, "To Build a Fire"

————, *The Call of the Wild*

Jacqueline Davies, *The Lemonade War*

Jacqueline Kelly, *The Evolution of Calpurnia Tate*

James Hurst, "The Scarlet Ibis"

James Thurber, "The Catbird Seat"

————, "Mr. Monroe Holds the Fort"

————, "The Unicorn in the Garden"

Jay Asher, *Thirteen Reasons Why*

Jean Craighead George, *Julie of the Wolves*

————, *My Side of the Mountain*

Jean Merrill, *The Pushcart War*

Jeanette Walls, *The Glass Castle*

Jerry Spinelli, *Maniac Magee*

Jhumpa Lahiri, *Unaccustomed Earth*

John F. Kennedy, *Profiles in Courage*

John Green, *Looking for Alaska*

————, *Paper Towns*

John Hersey, *Hiroshima*

John Steinbeck, *Cannery Row*

————, *The Graphes of Wrath*

————, *The Pearl*

————, *The Red Pony*

Joseph Krumgold, . . . *And Now Miguel*

————, *Onion John*

Judith Ortiz Coffer, "The Myth of the Latin Woman"

————, *Silent Dancing*

Kate Chopin, "A Respectable Woman"
Kate DiCamillo, *Because of Winn-Dixie*
————, *The Magician's Elephant*
————, *The Miraculous Journey*
————, *The Tiger Rising*
Kate Shelley, "Iowa Heroine"
Katherine Paterson, *Jacob Have I Loved*
————, *Park's Quest*
Kathleen O'Dell, *The Aviary*
Keith Donohue, *The Stolen Child*
Kelly Barnhill, *The Mostly True Story of Jack*
Kristin Cashore, *Fire*
Kurt Vonnegut, Jr. "Harrison Bergeron"
————, "How to Write with Style"
L. Frank Baum, *The Wonderful Wizard of Oz*
L. M. Montgomery, *Anne of Green Gables*
Larry McMurtry, *Lonesome Dove*
Laura Hillenbrand, *Seabiscuit*
————, *Unbroken*
Laura Ingalls Wilder, *Farmer Boy*
Laura Resau and Maria Virginia Farinango, *The Queen of Water*
Laurence E. Stotz, "Fire"
Laurence Yep, *Dragonwings*
Laurie Halse Anderson, *Speak*
Lemony Snicket, *A Series of Unfortunate Events*
Leon Hugo, "My Father and the Hippopotamus"
Leslie Morris, "Three Shots for Charlie Beston"
Liam O'Flaherty, "The Sniper"
Libba Bray, *A Great and Terrible Beauty*
Linda Sue Park, *A Single Shard*
Lisa Luedeke, *Smashed*
Lloyd Alexander, *The Book of Three*
Lois Duncan, *A Gift of Magic*

Lois Lenski, *Strawberry Girl*

Lois Lowry, *The Giver*

Louis Sachar, *Holes*

Lynne Rae Perkins, *Criss Cross*

Madeleine L'Engle, *A Wind in the Door*

————, *A Wrinkle in Time*

Maggie Stiefvater, *Forever*

Margaret Landon, *Anna and the King of Siam*

Marjorie Kinnan Rawlings, *The Yearling*

Megan Whalen Turner, *The King of Attolia*

Meindert DeJong, *The Wheel on the School*

Melina Marchetta, *Looking for Alibrandi*

Michael Crichton, *Jurassic Park*

————, *Travels*

Michael Morpurgo, *War Horse*

Michael Ondaatje, *Cat's Table*

Mildred D. Taylor, *Roll of Thunder, Hear My Cry*

Monica Sone, "The Japanese Touch"

Murray Heyert, "The New Kid"

Nancy Farmer, *The House of the Scorpion*

Naomi Hintze, "The Lost Gold Superstitions"

Natalie Babbitt, *Tuck Everlasting*

Neil Gaiman, *Coraline*

————, *The Graveyard Book*

Olive Ann Burns, *Cold Sassy Tree*

Orson Scott Card, *Ender's Game*

Otto H. Frank and Mirjam Pressler (editors), *The Diary of Anne Frank*

Patrick Ness, *A Monster Calls*

Paul Gallico, *The Snow Goose*

Paul Harding, *Tinkers*

Peter Abrahams, *Tell Freedom*

Philip Pullman, *The Golden Compass*

Phyllis Reynolds Naylor, *Shiloh*

Pierre Boulle, *Planet of the Apes*
Pierre Gascar, "The Little Square"
Rachel Carson, *The Edge of the Sea*
Ray Bradbury, "The Fog Horn"
———, *The Martian Chronicles*
———, "A Sound of Thunder"
Rebecca Skloot, *The Immortal Life of Henrietta Lacks*
Richard Adams, *Watership Down*
Richard Bach, *Jonathan Livingston Seagull*
Richard Connell, "The Most Dangerous Game"
Rick Riordan, *Heroes of Olympus*
———, *The Lightning Thief*
———, *The Throne of Fire*
Roald Dahl, *Fantastic Mr. Fox*
———, "The Great Grammatizator"
———, *James and the Giant Peach*
———, *Matilda*
Robert C. O'Brien, *Mrs. Frisby and the Rats of NIMH*
Robert Cormier, *Take Me Where the Good Times Are*
Robert Lipsyte, *The Contender*
Robert Ludlum, *The Moscow Vector*
———, *The Prometheus Deception*
Rosa Guy, *Edith Jackson*
———, *The Friends*
Sara Gruen, *Ape House*
Sarah Dessen, *Dreamland*
———, *Lock and Key*
———, *Someone Like You*
Saul Bellow, "A Father-to-Be"
Scott O'Dell, *Island of Blue Dolphins*
Scott Westerfeld, *Leviathan*
Sharon Creech, *Walk Two Moons*
Sharon M. Draper, *Out of My Mind*

Sheila Burnford, *The Incredible Journey*
Stephen Crane, "Horses—One Dash"
Stephen King, *Bag of Bones*
———, "The Body"
———, *The Eyes of the Dragon*
———, *Hearts in Atlantis*
———, *Needful Things*
———, *UR*
Stephenie Meyer, *Breaking Dawn*
———, *The Host*
———, *New Moon*
———, *Twilight*
Sue Monk Kidd, *The Secret Life of Bees*
Susan Cooper, *The Dark Is Rising*
———, *The Grey King*
Susan Fromberg Schaeffer, *Time in Its Flight*
Susan Patron, *The Higher Power of Lucky*
Suzanne Collins, *Catching Fire*
———, *The Hunger Games*
———, *Mockingjay*
Theodore Taylor, *The Cay*
Thomas Rockwell, *How to Eat Fried Worms*
Tom Wolfe, *A Man in Full*
Toni Cade Bambara, "Raymond's Run"
Toni Morrison, *Beloved*
Traci L. Jones, *Standing Against the Wind*
Tracy Chevalier, *The Girl with a Pearl Earring*
Tracy Kidder, *Home Town*
Truman Capote, *The Grass Harp*
Ved Mehta, "A Donkey in a World of Horses"
Virginia Hamilton, *M. C. Higgins, the Great*
W. W. Jacobs, "The Monkey's Paw"
Wallace Stegner, *Crossing to Safety*

Walter Dean Myers, *Motown and Didi*
Walter Lord, *A Night to Remember*
Warren St. John, *Outcasts United*
William E. Barrett, *The Lilies of the Field*
William Golding, *Lord of the Flies*
William H. Armstrong, *Sounder*
William Pène du Bois, *The Twenty-One Balloons*
William Stafford, "A Way of Writing"
Willie Morris, *My Dog Skip*
Wilson Rawls, *Where the Red Fern Grows*
Winston Churchill, "I Escape from the Boers"
Yann Martel, *Beatrice and Virgil*
———, *Life of Pi*

I can't stand a sentence until it sounds right, and I'll go over it again and again. Once the sentence rolls along in a certain way, that's sentence A. Sentence B may work out well, but then its effect on sentence A may spoil the rhythm of the two together. One of the long-term things about knitting a piece of writing together is making all this stuff fit.

—John McFee, author

In your writing, we hope all the stuff fits.

—Don and Jenny Killgallon, coauthors of this worktext
